InStyle

Secrets of Style

Secrets

The complete guide to dressing your best every day

Written by Lisa Arbetter

Illustrations by Monica Lind

# of Style

From the editors of In Style

Produced by Melcher Media
for In Style Books and Time Inc.
Home Entertainment

In Style
Managing Editor: Charla Lawhon
Executive Editors: Maria Baugh, Martha McCully
Design Director: Rip Georges
Photography Director: Laurie Kratochvil
Fashion Directors: Hal Rubenstein, Cynthia Weber Cleary
Market Director: Larissa Thomson
Market Editor: Toby Tucker
Style Editor: Sydne Bolden
Senior Accessories Editor: Alice H. Kim
Assoc. Accessories Editor: Erin Sumwalt

Editorial Director, Books: Mary Peacock
Vice President, Development: Amy Ford Keohane

President: Stephanie George
Publisher: Lynette Harrison Brubaker
General Manager: Maria Tucci
Director of Public Affairs: Sheri Lapidus
Associate Director of Public Affairs: Paul Reader
Marketing Manager: Lesley Osborn

Time Inc. Home Entertainment
Publisher: Richard Fraiman
Executive Director, Marketing Services: Carol Pittard
Director, Retail & Special Sales: Tom Mifsud
Marketing Director, Branded Businesses: Swati Rao
Assistant Financial Director: Steven Sandonato
Prepress Manager: Emily Rabin
Product Manager: Victoria Alfonso
Associate Book Production Manager: Suzanne Janso
Associate Prepress Manager: Anne-Michelle Gallero

Melcher Media
This book was produced by Melcher Media, Inc.,
124 West 13th Street, New York, NY 10011,
under the editorial direction of Charles Melcher.
www.melcher.com

Project Editor: John Meils
Assistant Editor: Megan Worman
Editorial Assistant: Allison Murray
Publishing Manager: Bonnie Eldon
Photo Researcher: Ellen Horan
Fashion Market Editor: Stacey Mayesh

Design by Pentagram.

Contents.

Foreword.

Our goals are to help you plan and shop for a wardrobe you love, so you'll always have something flattering (and comfortable) to put on, and to empower you to develop—and stick to—your own look.

The first thing to understand is that this is not a fashion book. Books, after all, are permanent—or as permanent as something printed on paper can be. Fashion, by its very definition, is constantly changing.

Style, however, is something else altogether, a distinctive way you speak, act or dress. (Have you noticed that some women have all three of these areas nailed?) Generally, we think of style as effortless—if you've got it, you must have been born with it.

In a word, Ha! While there's no doubt that style, or stylishness, comes easier to some than others, there is hope for us all. It's a matter of determining what works best for you. That said, we know that it's all too easy to get caught up in the latest-and-greatest, the hottest, the most of-the-moment trends, whether they are right for us or not. The truth is, trendiness hasn't won anyone a place on a best-dressed list—in Hollywood or in history.

Readers of this book may be familiar with *In Style,* but many of you may not. For nearly 10 years we've been covering the private side of Hollywood celebrities—especially the choices they make when it comes to beauty and fashion as the expression of their personal style. In editing the magazine month after month, we've worked with and interviewed the top style makers who help these stars look their best, in front of the cameras and in their private lives. Over the years the magazine's fashion coverage has grown under the talented hands and knowing eyes of *In Style*'s fashion directors, Hal Rubenstein and Cindy Weber Cleary, and their team. Making fashion understandable, achievable and, maybe most importantly, fun, has been their mission. To figure out how to make fashion work for each individual woman, no subject is considered too mundane: demystifying fit, from pants to jackets to bras to bathing suits; clarifying the right cuts for a particular figure; identifying flattering tones for your coloring.

Their ability to articulate the vision of *In Style*'s founding editor, Martha Nelson—that the magazine talks to the reader as a trusted friend—is evident every month, and now in this book: advising, not dictating, encouraging instead of admonishing, and, above all, being a reality-based style advisor that will cheer on its readers to embrace all the positive things fashion can do for them.

While many of us wouldn't mind looking like one of today's top stars (Julia Roberts, Jennifer Aniston or Reese Witherspoon, to name just a few)—women we cover every month in *In Style*—the truth of the matter is that we don't. We're taller or shorter. Our figures are bustier or more boyish. Our lives and lifestyles are not the same. What we *can* do is learn from their successes (or mistakes). We can analyze what works and what doesn't, and develop a personal style that is right for each of us.

One of the basic ideas that inspired the creation of the magazine is the notion that to be in style is to express yourself, to live with imagination, ease and confidence. And nowhere is that more true—and sometimes more difficult—than in the choices you make in dressing yourself.

And that's where *Secrets of Style* comes in. Its goals are to help you plan—and shop for—a wardrobe you love, so you'll always have something flattering (and comfortable) to put on, and to empower you to develop—and stick to—your own look. Here you'll find tips on exactly how clothes and accessories can be used to highlight your assets, how to focus on what's right for your body and your life, and, when it's called for, how to invest with assurance. Each piece of a basic wardrobe is analyzed, with suggestions for finding the details and styles that will best flatter your figure type. This advice is applicable to women of all shapes and sizes, but it must be taken for what it is: a starting point. Since everyone's body is different (long- or short-waisted, small- or large-busted, full- or narrow-hipped and so forth), you may find yourself fitting into more than one category. And because clothing comes in endless incarnations, not every suggestion will always work for you. We're providing guidelines, not definitive rules. Think of this book as a compass to point you in the right direction. After that, have fun experimenting.

While a book's worth of information may seem like an awful lot of thought to give to clothing (no matter how difficult finding the right pieces may be), the idea is that if you do a bit of strategizing up front, your life will be a lot easier on a daily basis. Or to put it another way, you'll have what you need when you need it. Rare will be the last minute, panicked run to the mall or department store in hopes of finding the right cocktail dress for your next party. And you may never again stand in front of a packed closet and say, "I've got nothing to wear!"

But perhaps the most important thing this book can give you is the confidence to pursue the style that works best for you. After reading through these pages, we hope you'll have a wardrobe that coordinates easily, fills your needs, flatters your figure and fits your body. And that you'll know which looks from a season's offerings will work best with what is already in your closet. Ultimately, we hope we can help you to look—and feel—your best every day.

Charla Lawhon
Managing Editor, In Style magazine

Style Secrets.

Basics.

> I have heard with admiring submission the experience of the lady who declared that the sense of being perfectly well dressed gives a feeling of inward tranquility which religion is powerless to bestow.
>
> RALPH WALDO EMERSON

Maybe it's a beautiful coat in a magazine spread, or a rerun of *Pillow Talk*, or a star giving an interview on TV, looking slim and smashing in the latest jeans. Regardless of what sets off your reverie, there's no denying that we all sometimes dream about being really well dressed. However, the trance usually doesn't last long. Then our thoughts might wander to our wallet, our thighs or our busy schedule, and we dismiss the idea of being chic as something reserved for the very rich or the very thin. But money and an enviable set of gams do not a well-dressed woman make. Plenty of women who are on a tight budget or think they have figure problems still manage to look wonderful every day. That's because they've learned the real secret of style: Know what suits you. So take a moment to learn how to use your clothes to showcase what's most beautiful about *you* and how to add the personal touches that make a look your own. Soon you, too, will be on your way to leading a perfectly well-dressed life.

Jennifer Aniston's outfit, though simple in shape and color, is stunning. And here's the best part: It's slimming, too.

FIGURE FLATTERY 101

Dressing with style involves more than just wearing what you like. It takes strategy. By using your clothing's fit, fabric, color, details, pattern and proportions to lengthen, slim and direct attention to exactly where you want it (and away from the places you don't), you'll be able to create a look that is both flattering and in keeping with your personality.

Fit.

Everything you wear should fit perfectly. This may seem obvious, but who hasn't stood in front of a dressing room mirror and convinced herself that no one else will notice that the skirt (or dress, or blouse) is just a tiny bit too tight? News flash: That dastardly duo—puckering fabric and a strained seam—will give you away every time. Good fit means that clothes skim the body (showing curves without clinging to them) and that all the details (lapels, pocket flaps, slits, seams and pleats) lie flat. Any time clothing pulls or buckles, it not only creates a sloppy appearance, but adds pounds. The same negative effects are true for garments that are too big. In the following chapters, you'll learn what a tailor can do for you and that sweating the small stuff—adjusting a skirt hem, the length of a jacket, or the width of a sleeve—can make a big difference in your overall appearance.

The perfect fit of Nicole Kidman's dress is key to her sophisticated style.

Fabric.

Fabrics that fall smoothly over the curves of your body are the most flattering. But the hunt for just the right drape, weight and texture can take some patience. If a fabric is too stiff, it takes on a shape of its own and winds up looking boxy; too thin, and it clings to every bump and bulge; too bulky or too shiny, and it adds pounds. Just right is a matte fabric free of unwanted heft but with enough body to slide over problem areas. Fabrics like wool crepe, wool-microfiber blends, cotton or wool gabardine, cotton blended with silk, flat knits, two-ply silks and some synthetics are good choices, depending on the garment. (See below for more on how to match fabrics and garments for the best look.) A touch of spandex helps, too; three to five percent is usually plenty—any more, and you'll look like you belong in an aerobics class.

FABRICS: A PRIMER

The adage "you get what you pay for" is gospel with fabric. Cheap fabrics tend to be stiff and less flattering. Higher-quality fabrics look better, last longer and hold their shape better. Many factors determine the quality of fabric: the fibers; how they're spun into yarns; how the yarn is woven or knitted into a fabric; and any finishes applied.

Most fabrics fall into two categories: knitted or woven. Knits, the more flexible of the two, are best suited for body-contouring styles, like sweaters or T-shirts. Woven fabrics are stronger and hold form better, but because they are less flexible than knits, need a lot of tailoring for a perfect fit. Tightly woven fabrics (like denim) are preferable for heartier, semi-fitted fare, while loosely woven fabrics (like chiffon) are better for loose-fitting, gathered garments or ones that drape.

Color.

As anyone who has ever stepped out of the house in a red dress knows, color catches the eye and can make you look terrific. (See Page 19 to find the best shades for you.) Here are some ways to harness color's formidable power:

Monochromatic. There are two compelling reasons to dress in one color, head to toe: The long, unbroken line it creates makes for a pulled-together look, and an overall color can actually make you appear slimmer. Stark color contrasts draw the eye and form horizontal lines that divide your body, making it appear wider and shorter. If you've got a little belly bulge, for example, the line created where your white shirt hits your black pants calls attention to that very spot. A monochromatic look, however, helps the eye glide right over trouble spots. It's this illusion that makes one-color dressing the backbone of many a stylish woman's wardrobe. And while you can achieve the effect with any color, darker shades, which absorb light, are the most slimming. But this doesn't mean being relegated to a dark, drab life. As long as there is a long, unbroken line on the outside (made by a suit, for example) or on the inside (with a top and skirt of one color and a jacket or cardigan of another color), the benefit remains. You can also add vibrancy without breaking the line by playing with different textures—a nubby tweed skirt with a silk shirt is one way— or by dressing in different tones of the same color (like black with charcoal gray, midnight blue with navy, or hunter green with forest).

By pairing different tones of the same color, Elizabeth Hurley proves that monochromatic dressing is far from boring.

Bright and light colors. Even though dark colors can make you appear slimmer, and lighter, brighter colors can do the opposite, there is still a place for vivid hues in your wardrobe. By strategically placing paler or brightly colored pieces near or over a part of your body that you like, you're making sure it gets the attention it deserves. You can also pair brights with darks to balance your body. If you're small on top and heavier on the bottom, for example, a hot pink T-shirt worn with a black skirt will give you a more proportioned look (as long as the line created by the divide between the pieces lands over one of your leaner parts).

Natalie Portman showcases her bottom half by wearing brightly colored slacks with a dark top.

Details and flourish.

Details, color and naked skin can be used to divert attention to a place you'd rather emphasize. So by all means use your cleavage to draw attention away from an ample derrière, or wear a skirt with an embroidered hem to draw the eye to your gorgeous legs. Just be wary of too much of a good thing. Excessive detailing does more than just create questionable overall looks—it dates your clothes, eats into their versatility and makes you look heavier. Anything that adds an additional layer or girth—ruffles, patch pockets, wide lapels, big buttons or epaulettes—only accentuates what's underneath. There's also the danger of unwittingly adding horizontal lines to your outfits. For example, if you were to try on a safari jacket (with all of the horizontals created by its belt and numerous pockets) and a single-breasted pocketless jacket, the simple blazer would give you a much slimmer appearance, because it contains no details that add bulk and distract the eye from its straight up-and-down path.

The ruffled hem of Renée Zellweger's dress draws attention to her gorgeous gams.

A medium-sized, multicolored print flatters Angie Harmon's tall and slender frame.

Pattern.

With pattern, there are four considerations: color, size, direction and the subtleties of stripes.

Color. Tonal patterns (pink on red, say) attract less attention than those in contrasting colors, and the darker the background, the more slimming the print.

Size. Always choose prints that are in scale with your size. Petite figures are more flattered by small, low-contrast prints (like a small olive polka dot on a hunter background), while taller women can take bigger prints with more contrast (like a bold red-and-blue floral on a white background). Large women should also choose bigger prints, but may benefit more from the slimming power of a low-contrast design. A uniform, all-over pattern, which keeps the eye from resting on any one spot, is also a good diversionary tactic for voluptuous bodies.

Direction. Sometimes the print itself creates a line, and sometimes the negative space does it. Either way, vertical lines are preferable to horizontal lines, and diagonal lines that are more vertical than horizontal will have the same elongating effect as a true vertical.

Stripes. When it comes to wearing stripes, the decision involves more than simply choosing between horizontal or vertical lines. While it's generally true that verticals lengthen and slim and that some horizontals will make a heavy area look heavier, it all depends on the size and spacing of the stripe. Horizontals *can* be used to create beneficial optical illusions if you're of average size. Widely placed horizontal stripes, for example, can give the illusion of a bigger bust and—when worn with a dark bottom—can help balance a pear-shaped figure. If the horizontals are thin and widely spaced, they can have a lengthening effect, while widely spaced vertical stripes can widen. No matter which way your stripes fall, however, make sure the garment is on the loose side. If it's too tight or stretchy, you'll wind up wearing squiggles!

Proportion.

Figure flattery is not just about camouflage and diversion—it's also a balancing act. The length of your legs in relation to your torso, the width of your shoulders in relation to your hips—these things matter to your overall appearance, and, just like everything else, they can be manipulated.

Generally, to avoid cutting your body right through the middle horizontally, every outfit should be either "short-over-long" (or full) or "long-over-short" (or narrow). A short jacket over an A-line skirt or a cropped jacket over trousers is one way to achieve the short-over-long look. Conversely, a long jacket with skinny pants or a tunic over a pencil skirt creates a long-over-short (or narrow) outfit. After that, you need to work with your own proportions.

Are you short-waisted (short torso, longer legs) or long-waisted (long torso, shorter legs)? To find out, measure the distance between your bottom rib and the top of your hipbone. If it's just a few inches, you are short-waisted; four or more inches, and you are long-waisted. Once you know, you want to wear a waistband that balances you out: If you are short-waisted, look for a lower waistline, and if you are long-waisted, look for a higher one.

A short jacket over a longer skirt makes Cindy Crawford's silhouette even leggier.

Find your figure.

This chart outlines some general guidelines for dealing with common figure problems. These are not hard and fast rules. Everyone's body is different, so experiment and adapt as you see fit.

Curvy

GOAL:
Showcasing your waist, elongating your figure and showing off your curves without over-emphasizing them.

STOCK UP ON:
Pieces that fall smoothly over your curves.

Pieces that are nipped at the waist and narrow at the knee.

Tops that reveal skin at the shoulder, collarbone or cleavage.

Skirts and dresses with slits to show your legs.

Jackets with a top button right under the bust.

Slim-cut pants.

Monochromatic separates.

Pieces that incorporate vertical detailing.

Outfits with clean lines.

Wrap-style blouses and dresses.

STEER CLEAR OF:
Anything oversized.

Anything too tight.

Very thin fabrics.

Clothes that are cut straight up-and-down.

Jackets that button loosely at the waist.

Tops and jackets that end at the fullest part of your hips.

Short

GOAL:
Elongating your legs and creating a strong vertical line from head to toe.

STOCK UP ON:
Monochromatic outfits.

Fluid fabrics.

High-waisted tops and dresses.

Anything that adds vertical lines, including princess seams, a center seam down the front or back and high closures.

Minimal accessories, all in proportion to your body.

Medium-height heels.

STEER CLEAR OF:
Stiffly tailored clothes.

Tops that hit at the waistline.

Horizontals.

Pleated trousers.

Midcalf-length skirts.

Anything baggy.

Cropped pants.

Anything that could make you look little-girlish—ruffles, bows or other "sweet" details

Narrow Shoulders

GOAL:
Squaring your shoulders and creating balance between your hips and shoulders.

STOCK UP ON:
Shoulder pads.

Tops with shoulder detailing like epaulettes or yokes.

Tops with horizontal lines or patterns.

Boatneck tops or those with a wide V-necks.

Collared shirts.

Tops with breast pockets and lapels.

Structured, tailored styles.

Tops and jackets with set-in sleeves, placed slightly outside the shoulder bone.

STEER CLEAR OF:
Raglan sleeves (with seams running diagonally from under the arms in toward the neck).

Look five pounds thinner by pairing slim-fitting monochromatic separates with a fitted, knee-length jacket.

Broad Shoulders

GOAL:
Softening your shoulders.

STOCK UP ON:
Raglan sleeves.

Set-in sleeves that do not exceed your shoulder bones.

Dark tops.

Deep V-neck tops.

If you're also slim-hipped, choose skirts or bottoms with horizontal patterns or detailing, to balance your figure.

STEER CLEAR OF:
Epaulettes.

Shoulder pads.

Horizontal lines at the shoulders, including seams.

Boatneck tops.

Color-blocking over your shoulders.

Shirts made of shiny fabrics.

Blouses with puffy sleeves.

Full Bust

GOAL:
Showing your curves without over-emphasizing them, and elongating your torso and neck.

STOCK UP ON:
Dark-toned tops, lighter bottoms.

Uncomplicated tops.

Open-neck sweaters, blouses and dresses.

Collars that are long, vertical and narrow.

Anything that adds a vertical line above the waist or a flourish below it.

STEER CLEAR OF:
Double-breasted styles.

Wide belts.

Collars with large lapels.

Anything that adds bulk around the neck.

Tops or jackets made from stiff fabrics.

Baggy tops.

Bulky knits.

Tops with large patterns.

Small Bust

GOAL:
Showcasing the curves you've got.

STOCK UP ON:
Push-up bras, if you're interested in enhancement.

Tops and dresses with horizontal lines and flourishes over the bust.

Tops, jackets and dresses with breast pockets.

Fitted tops and jackets.

Wide lapels and collars.

Empire-waist dresses and tops.

Halter tops.

STEER CLEAR OF:
Loose or overly structured tops.

Stiff fabrics.

Heavy Arms

GOAL:
Slimming and elongating your arms and torso.

STOCK UP ON:
Tops with sleeves that taper to the wrist.

Long-sleeve tops or those that end just above the elbow.

Raglan, dolman and kimono sleeves (or any that allow extra room in the armhole).

Tops with quiet verticals, like seams or a long, thin lapel.

STEER CLEAR OF:
Tight tops and sleeves.

Tops made out of stiff fabrics.

Sleeveless or very short-sleeve tops.

Tummy

GOAL:
Refocusing attention from your middle to your legs or face, and creating one long vertical.

STOCK UP ON:
Long tops like tunics, cardigans, jackets and shirts that don't tuck in.

Fabrics that drape but don't cling.

Flat-front or side-zip pants and skirts.

Monochromatic outfits.

Jackets and tops that are nipped at the waist.

Empire-waist tops and dresses.

Narrow pants—if you have slim hips and legs.

Sheath dresses that skim the body.

Single-breasted coats.

STEER CLEAR OF:
Belted dresses and tops.

Belts in bright colors or with lots of flourish—like embroidery, hand-painting or metal studs.

Tops with waistbands or anything that cinches.

Cropped tops.

Pants or skirts with any waist detailing or pockets.

Bias cuts.

Pinstripes and a thin, narrow lapel enhance the slimming powers of a lean pantsuit.

Short-Waisted/Long Legs

GOAL:
Creating the illusion of a lower waistline and refocusing attention from your middle to your face or legs.

STOCK UP ON:
Monochromatic outfits.

Lower-waisted bottoms.

Longer shirts and jackets.

Tops with vertical lines.

Narrow hip belts.

Narrow belts that match your top.

STEER CLEAR OF:
Anything that slices at the waist.

Wide waistbands or belts.

Anything high-waisted.

Long-Waisted/Short Legs

GOAL:
Creating the illusion of a higher waistline and longer legs.

STOCK UP ON:
Higher-waisted garments.

Cuffless trousers.

Trousers with slim legs, cut a little longer.

Heeled, slim shoes toned to match bottoms.

Pantyhose toned to match bottoms and shoes.

Belts that match your bottoms.

STEER CLEAR OF:

Anything that cuts off the length of your legs.

Low-waisted anything.

Patterned hose.

Bottom Heavy

GOAL:
Showing your curves without over-emphasizing them, elongating your figure and balancing your shoulders and hips.

STOCK UP ON:
Close-fitting tops that float over hips and derrière.

Tailored jackets with nipped waistlines that just cover the hips or stop at the top of the hipbone.

Dark-colored bottoms.

Lower-waisted bottoms, which de-emphasize the curve of the hips.

Dark, tapered skirts in soft, drape-friendly fabrics.

Straight-leg, flat-front trousers.

If you're pear-shaped, tops with horizontal stripes or shoulder pads.

Tonal outfits with the deeper shade on the bottom.

STEER CLEAR OF:
Bottoms or dresses made of clingy fabrics.

Bottoms with any horizontal lines.

Drawstring pants.

Shiny fabrics or thick textures on your bottom half.

Bottoms with lots of pleats, gathers, back details, back pockets or big prints.

Tops that stop at the waist or mid-hips.

Anything that hits at the widest part of your hips.

Anything boxy.

Anything that cinches the waist.

FIND YOUR COLORS

Ever have one of those days when people keep commenting on how radiant and well-rested you look? Unless you've just returned from a two-week jaunt in the Caribbean, chances are you've hit upon a flattering color. The right color can do wonders, brightening your eyes and evening out your skin tone. The wrong color will have you reaching for your makeup.

The colors that best suit you depend on your skin tone and the color of your hair and eyes. To discover your best colors, there are various cosmetic programs that can help, but with a bit of attention and patience, you can easily judge by yourself. Simply experiment with lots of different colors, always examining yourself in daylight against a white background. (Artificial lighting and the presence of other colors change a color's tone.) If you're trying on a color in a store without windows, take the piece home. You can always return it if it's unflattering. When you hit on a color that is right, you'll know immediately.

Also, remember that colors come in many tones. Just because you look sallow in an orangy-red doesn't mean that all reds are out of the question. Try a brick red or a garnet red. Once you find one that works, chances are you'll be able to wear that same tone in other colors as well. For example, if you find that you can wear the garnet red but not a brick red, than you'll have a better chance with an emerald than an olive green. Overall, you're going to find many wearable colors—but, in the interest of saving money and building a coordinating wardrobe, you'll be better off limiting yourself to two neutrals and three or four bright colors.

BEYOND THE BASICS

Think of figure flattery as Dressing 101 and developing your style as something more advanced. Now that you've mastered the basics, follow these three simple steps and take what you've learned to the next level.

Step 1: Play up your strengths.

Great legs, a beautiful face, sexy cleavage, perfect shoulders, a long neck, fabulous hair—whatever features you love about yourself need to be highlighted by your outfit. Shine, pattern, bright and light colors, details and skin all attract the eye—so use them to showcase your assets, just as these famous women do.

Sarah Jessica Parker chose a spaghetti-strap dress to showcase her buff biceps.

This dress is deceptively simple—but Salma Hayek's curves make it sizzle.

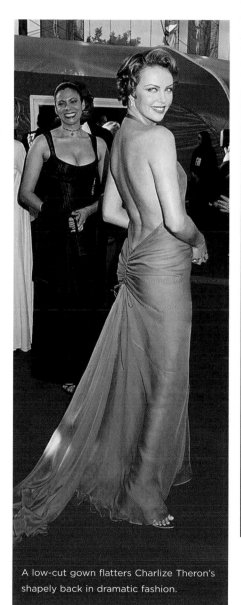

A low-cut gown flatters Charlize Theron's shapely back in dramatic fashion.

Cameron Diaz has got legs—and in this short dress, she shows them off to great effect.

The diagonal line on this curve-hugging skirt puts the focus firmly on Jennifer Lopez's sexy hips.

Step 2: Develop a signature look.

Virginia Woolf once said, "Vain trifles as they seem, clothing...change[s] our view of the world and the world's view of us." Since people tend to form initial opinions by appearance, give them a taste of what they're looking for—the real you. You can do this in small ways, as the women here have done, by always wearing your favorite color or accessory. Or go even further and develop a full uniform based on whatever it is that makes you feel your best. Whether it's a chic pantsuit or a flirty dress, wearing some variation of it every day of the year isn't boring—it's just very you.

Cate Blanchett favors pieces enriched by beautiful details like beadwork and fine embroidery.

Gabrielle "Coco" Chanel made strands and strands of pearls part of her personal style.

Reese Witherspoon gravitates toward dresses and skirts with a vintage, lady-like flair.

Step 3: And don't underestimate...

Good posture. Mother *does* know best: Lifting your head and letting your shoulders drop back and down is the single simplest thing you can do for yourself. It makes you look taller, thinner, more elegant and more confident. So heed Mom's words, and stand up straight!

A great haircut. A good haircut can do as much for you as a good vacation. It brightens your eyes, makes your face prettier and can definitely make you look younger. Yes, good haircuts can be expensive, but what they add to overall appearance makes them worth every penny. Since your hair is front and center, get a cut you can manage at all times—not one that looks good only when a professional styles it. It's also a good idea to have an emergency styling plan for nasty weather and one for those days when you're overdue for your next trim.

Confidence. Many of the most attractive people in the world are not the most stylish. But they radiate a self-assurance and sense of calm that act like a magnet and get them noticed no matter what they're wearing.

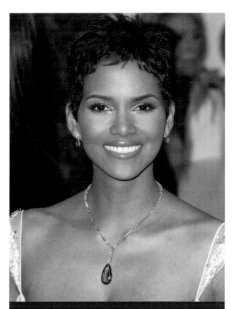

Halle Berry's short, spiky hairstyle is a great foil for her very feminine face.

Gwen Stefani fearlessly mixes a designer skirt with a T-shirt and—even—a wrist sweatband.

Heather Locklear's beautiful posture makes her—and her clothes—look even better.

Classics.

Audrey Hepburn stuck to classic shapes, which is why her simple, chic look still takes the breath away.

> All a woman needs to be chic is a raincoat, two suits, a pair of trousers and a cashmere sweater.
>
> HUBERT DE GIVENCHY

The Audrey Hepburn classic *Breakfast at Tiffany*'s continues to enchant us more than forty years after its release. And a big part of the film's romance has to do with Audrey Hepburn's fantastic wardrobe. The two chic black dresses, the belted trench, and the low-heel, pointy pumps look incredibly stylish—even today—because the clothes' designer, Hubert de Givenchy, believed in clean lines and restraint.

Givenchy's message of simplicity is the essence of timeless design. It's the reason a look endures, not only for seasons, but for decades. Trends, on the other hand, are mercurial by nature. Chasing them is not only exhausting and expensive, but the payoff—a fleeting moment of hipness followed by a lifetime of groaning at old photos—is pretty paltry, too. That isn't to say that trendy items have no place in the wardrobe of a well-dressed woman. But they should be used sparingly, like seasoning, so they complement a wardrobe of your favorite classics without ever overwhelming them.

CLASSICS THROUGH THE AGES

Before you look ahead to what the gods of fashion will deem the next hot item, take a moment to look back over the years. You'll see that really well-designed clothes are eternally chic.

Trench coat.

1948
Marlene Dietrich in
A Foreign Affair.

1963
Brigitte Bardot shopping on
London's Regent Street.

1979
Meryl Streep in *Kramer v.
Kramer.*

1993
Madonna in *Body
of Evidence.*

Turtleneck.

1945
Lauren Bacall.

1965
Sophia Loren in
Operation Crossbow.

1970
Ali McGraw.

2002
Reese Witherspoon in
Sweet Home Alabama.

Pencil skirt.

1946
Lena Horne in *Till the Clouds Roll By.*

1952
Marilyn Monroe on the streets of Hollywood.

1980s
Linda Evans on the set of "Dynasty."

2003
Drew Barrymore at Grauman's Chinese Theatre in Hollywood.

Blazer.

1939
Bette Davis.

1955
Jane Russell on location shooting *The Revolt of Mamie Stover.*

1980
Lauren Hutton.

1994
Julia Roberts in *I Love Trouble.*

SIX FIGURE-FLATTERING CLASSICS NO CLOSET SHOULD BE WITHOUT

Fitted cotton shirt

Straight-cut, knee-length coat

Flat-front, straight-leg pant

Flesh-colored pump

Straight-cut turtleneck

Semi-fitted, two-button jacket

Trend management.

There's no denying it: Buying and wearing a trendy item can be a rush. It gives your wardrobe a shot of the new and helps you look and feel hip. But don't get carried away. While one trend may have you looking in sync with the times, two or more can have you suddenly looking like a fashion victim. Follow these guidelines to get just the right touch of trendiness every time.

One piece is plenty. Really. There is no need to go out and buy yourself a new wardrobe every season. By simply pairing a T-shirt in the latest color or a skirt in the newest shape with one of the more classic items you already own, you'll instantly get a fresh look.

Choose a trendy shape or a trendy color—never both. You want the biker jacket *or* pink, not the pink biker jacket. Avoid trend overload.

Wear only those trends that suit you. By all means, if red is the color of the season and it looks great on you, stock up—but if the hip new color happens to be a sallow-inducing pea green, better to go without. Remember, it's sticking to what makes you look and feel great that makes you the ultimate in chic.

THE COST-PER-WEAR CONCEPT

Classic clothing is classic because it can be worn for years without looking dated. That makes it a great value—if you get pieces that are built to last. To do so, you'll have to spend a little extra to buy the highest quality you can afford. While this can be justified in the abstract, it's harder to stomach when looking at a price tag. So calm down by remembering that with well-made classics, unlike trendy items, the cost per wear is much lower—the more you wear something, the less expensive it becomes. If a black cashmere turtle-neck and a pink ruffled blouse cost the same, the turtleneck is the better value; you'll get so much more use out of it.

Debra Messing pairs her of-the-moment mini with a classic turtleneck.

Penelope Cruz updates her classic jeans with a chain belt.

Milla Jovovich adds an au courant color to her black skirt and boots staples.

Shopping.

Alicia Silverstone's character in *Clueless* indulges in some serious retail therapy.

> Style is very different from fashion. Once you find something that works, keep it.
>
> TOM FORD, GUCCI

When it comes to shopping, most women fall into one of two camps: those who love it and those who find it about as appealing as scrubbing the bathtub. For the "anti-shoppers," even thinking about a mall run raises the worst fears: The harsh dressing-room light that raises body-image paranoia to new heights; price tags that make dollar signs ka-ching in front of the eyes; or finding nothing but obscenely trendy items that bring back memories of the dark parts of the closet where the mini-kilts, floral culottes and other fashion skeletons reside. Whatever the worry, making time to shop is not a top priority for this group. The result: A wardrobe of make-do pieces that neither excite the wearer nor make her look great. Members of the pro-shopping camp, on the other hand, have no problem carving out time for a little recreational shopping. Their downfall is usually impulse buying, and that leads to a disjointed wardrobe of throwaway pieces that the wearer quickly retires out of boredom.

No matter which group of shoppers you fall into (or if you're somewhere in between), you can quell angst and refrain from frivolous spending by being more systematic in your approach. First, plan your excursions—decide ahead of time exactly what items you're looking for and how much you can spend. Next, focus while you're there, so you'll get clothing that flatters your figure and works into your life. Finally, invest in top-quality pieces that will last. Follow these three simple steps, and before you know it, your closet will be filled with clothes you actually want to be seen in.

THREE STEPS TO SHOPPING SUCCESS

Step 1: Plan.

Take stock of what you already have and what you need. Start by trying on all of those items in your closet that aren't part of your weekly rotation. Throw out anything that's worn; give away anything that's dated; and decide if the pieces with a less-than-perfect fit can be saved by a tailor. Also think back on those rushed mornings when you're trying to get dressed and out of the house. What is it that you're always reaching for but never seem to have? A straight black skirt? A middle-weight jacket? Make a list of the things you need to replace or fill in, and then set priorities.

Determine the amount you can spend. Credit card debt is not chic. Make sure that you set aside enough money to get what you need without spending more than you can afford. Remember, for example, that most winter clothing costs more than summer wear, so plan accordingly.

Shop only when you're feeling good about yourself. Stepping into a store when you're feeling down presents two dangers. The first is the shopping blackout, which happens when you start buying just for the thrill of it without any thought at all. While it may feel good at the moment, this type of joy is fleeting, and dread awaits you when you spy that pile of receipts on your dresser the following morning. The other danger is self-loathing. When you're not feeling your best, standing naked amid a pile of castoffs under harsh lighting and in front of a mirror can do terrible things to your self-esteem. Why put yourself through that?

Dress comfortably. Wear lightweight clothes that are easy to get in and out of, like pants, sweaters and slip-on shoes. Pantyhose should be left at home unless you're trying on something that you would normally wear with hose, like a skirt or dress. Wear plain panties and a smooth bra to avoid distracting lines and creases when trying on tighter-fitting pieces. If what you're shopping for requires a specific undergarment—say, a strapless bra or a shaper—bring it along. And last, make sure you do a little something with your hair and makeup. You don't need to hit the mall made-up for a black-tie event, but look nice. It will help you get a better idea of how great you'll look in the clothes you're trying on.

Shop when the stores are least crowded. Try early in the week, or early in the morning. Saturdays are when stores see their biggest crowds, so if you must go on a Saturday, go very early in the morning or later in the evening.

Give yourself time. This is a two-pronged piece of advice. Part one is: Don't wait until the last minute to buy something you need. This is a common mistake when it comes to special-occasion dressing. If you're the type of person who plans ahead, you'll already have on hand a black-tie dress, an interview outfit and something to wear to a wedding. If you don't have the necessary outfit in your wardrobe, start hunting at least a month before a special event. Second, leave your shopping day wide open. Don't squeeze your shopping into your lunch hour or between appointments. You need time to search, try on and ponder.

USING A PERSONAL SHOPPER

Personal shopping is a service often provided for free by high-end department stores. These shoppers search the store and pick out clothes for you and have them waiting when you get there. It's a great time saver, but there is no guarantee that you will immediately find a shopper who understands your taste and needs. That's why it's a good idea to meet with one beforehand. Be very clear about your likes and dislikes, your budget and your particular needs.

A good personal shopper has gained extensive experience from dressing women of all shapes, ages and sizes. Like a good hairdresser, she will consider what you've said, but she'll also put her expertise to work for you by offering up a few ideas of her own. The downside of the department store personal shopper is that you are limited to the selections in one store. You could either employ the services of a number of different shoppers in several stores or hire an independent personal shopper. While the latter can be quite expensive—$100 per hour or more—personal shoppers also do a lot more legwork by running to stores all over town, including those you've never heard of.

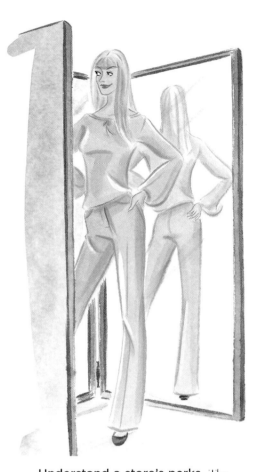

Understand a store's perks. The levels of service differ greatly by store. Department stores and big national chains offer a huge selection and loads of inventory, personal shopping services, longer return policies, and tailoring. Discount stores usually have liberal return policies and a huge selection, but because they keep prices down by lowering store overhead, there is little help and the sales floor is often cluttered. In a boutique, you'll usually find more knowledgeable salespeople—along with a selection of unique offerings that reveal a very specific sense of style.

Familiarize yourself with the store's return policy. Two weeks is standard. Large department stores usually allow more time (up to 30 days), as do national chains and discount outlets. Many smaller boutiques, however, offer only store credit. The policy is usually posted in the shop or printed on the receipt, but you should always ask before you pay—especially when buying sale items, which often cannot be returned at all.

Step 2: Focus.

Shop alone. This is the only way to ensure that the focus remains firmly on you and your particular needs. Of course, if you love shopping with your friends, just make sure they understand that you're on a mission to find something specific. Don't let them mess with your convictions. If you know something is wrong for you, leave it behind.

Focus on what works for you.

Never give up on a sure thing. You know the shapes and colors that look good on you, so zero in on them. Of course, this doesn't mean you shouldn't experiment. Just keep in mind what you already know about flattering cuts, colors, fabrics and styles that will enhance your figure and coloring.

Try on clothes in front of a three-way mirror.

Contorting your body so you can see your backside isn't enough. You want to see your clothing as it will really look—and the only way to do that is in front of a three-way mirror. It helps you to ensure a perfect fit and allows you to better judge the quality of the clothing. (See Page 35 for more info on how to determine quality.)

Buy for the body you've got, not the one you want.

Even if you're planning to lose a little weight, it's still crucial to follow this advice: Buying clothes that are too snug will only make you appear heavier. You can always have something taken in later when you've accomplished your weight-loss goal. In any case, the idea is to look good *now*, and you will—even with that extra five pounds—if your clothes fit you to a T.

Buy for your real life. You want your clothes to allow you to be comfortable and to let you move with ease through your life. Don't let a friend talk you out of flats or kitten heels if that's what works for you—even if your friend won't step out of her house wearing anything less than a three-inch heel. Trust your instincts—because if you don't want the heels and buy them anyway, under pressure, you probably won't ever feel like putting them on. A large part of being chic is being comfortable. If you're in pain or you don't feel like yourself, it's going to show.

Don't compromise. As a day of shopping wears on, it gets more and more tempting just to buy something—anything—to avoid feeling as if you've wasted a day. But ask yourself this: Is leaving with something you're only going to wind up returning really the best way to make up for lost time?

Speak up. Find a knowledgeable saleswoman (look for someone dressed with style) and talk to her. Give her a clear sense of what you're looking for; she can become a terrific ally in your search for the most flattering, stylish clothes in the store. You can tap into her knowledge of what's on the sales floor. Find out if the pieces you're trying on have any mates—if not at the store you're in, then perhaps at another branch. Ask the saleswoman if the store provides tailoring services and, if not, whether she can recommend a tailor. Even ask her opinion—just don't let her advice overrule your own instincts. Seek out the same sales rep whenever you're in the store. Chances are, she might even call you when new merchandise is in and let you know when the store is having a sale.

Step 3: Invest.

Buy complete outfits. If you're trying on a jacket and it's got matching pants—or better yet, pants and a skirt—buy them. Now you've got two suits and three separate pieces that can be worked into other outfits—a find that's sure to simplify your morning routine. Even if the piece you're looking at isn't being shown with any others, take time to hunt for something to wear with it, so it doesn't just hang in your closet waiting for a mate. If you're shopping for something to go with a piece you've already got at home, bring a swatch or the entire garment, so you can make sure it's a good match.

Buy in multiples. The pants that fit your derrière just so, the T-shirt that feels smooth against your skin and falls close to the body, a dress that makes you look impossibly tall—these rare and wonderful items deserve to be bought in every color you can find.

Buy the best quality that you can afford. Invest in those pieces that you will wear time and again—the neutral suit, the black pants, the cashmere sweater set, the sheath dress. You'll get a better fit, finer fabrics and—overall—a nicer-looking garment that will elevate the look of the less expensive items you pair with it. Yes, it can be tough to choose a cashmere sweater that costs twice as much as one in wool, but in the end, it's an investment that will pay off. You'll need fewer garments because better-quality clothes are generally more durable and versatile, and you'll always feel your best—which, in itself, is priceless.

Be wary of the siren call of the sale rack. A great price can be tempting—but just because something has been marked down to an alluringly cheap price doesn't make it fit better or go with anything in your wardrobe. A bargain is only a bargain if it's something you will actually wear.

Buy classics and build on them. Spend first on the basic items in solid colors. They are the most versatile, so you'll never again feel like you have nothing to wear. Remember: To look great, you don't need a totally new outfit every day of the week. No one will notice if you wear your basic black pants on both Monday and Thursday. After you've invested in your simple shapes and neutrals, start filling in with pieces that are more memorable. And then, when you do come across something you really love—even if you can't see wearing it every week or even every month—you won't need to deny yourself. As long as it fits you perfectly and you feel comfortable in it, you'll find a place for it in your wardrobe.

SPENDING TIP

If your budget won't allow for all high-quality pieces, scrimp on the darks. Workmanship is much more noticeable on a garment that is made of a light-colored fabric, so inexpensive light-colored pieces will always look cheaper than inexpensive dark-colored ones.

TELLTALE SIGNS OF QUALITY

Most people rely on price and a designer label to put their mind at ease about the quality of a garment. Neither, however, is a risk-free indicator. The real story is in a garment's manufacture. So instead of looking at *who* made a garment, look at *how* it was made to make sure you're getting what you're paying for.

Hems. A good hem is double-stitched and invisible from the outside of the garment. A generous hem allowance is also a good sign.

Seams. All seams should lie straight without pulling or puckering and, preferably, be generous enough to let out if the need arises.

Stitching. It should be secure and straight. Look for about eight to 12 stitches per inch.

Linings. They should be made of smooth fabrics like rayon, acetate or silk. If the lining fabric is stiff, it will ruin the drape of the clothing.

Buttons. The buttons should match the garment, meet the buttonhole perfectly, be sewn on securely and, on heavier fabrics, reinforced with disks. Buttonholes should be perfectly finished, with no loose threads.

Zippers. They should be hidden and dyed to match the garment. Pull them up and down a few times to make sure they work smoothly without snagging.

Patterns. Printed and woven patterns should match up on all seams. If it's a two-piece outfit, patterns should always match up from piece to piece.

SHOPPING THE SALES

The basics that are the backbone of a chic wardrobe are usually long gone by clearance time—but that doesn't mean you shouldn't look. However, sales are more fruitful if you're after novelty or luxury items—like a sweater in a color you would not normally buy, or a beaded evening bag, or for picking up another version of something you've already got. Department stores have sales year-round, but the deepest markdowns can be found at the end of the fall and spring seasons. Specialty boutiques follow their own sale schedules. Get on the mailing lists of your favorite stores to receive advance notice of sales.

FALL AND WINTER MERCHANDISE
Cold-weather clothes usually start to go on sale in October, with final markdowns starting after Christmas and going through January and February.

Coats. Winter coats are marked down starting in January.

SPRING AND SUMMER MERCHANDISE
First markdowns are in April. August brings final markdowns. Back-to-school sales start in July and August.

Swimsuits. Swimwear is marked down after Memorial Day.

VINTAGE CLOTHES

Ah, the olden days, when clothes were hand-made and fabrics were of tip-top quality. Shopping for vintage clothes gives you access to beautifully made garments—and buying them allows you the thrill of being uniquely dressed—but it also offers another, often over-looked, benefit: a century of silhouettes. Say you're a long-waisted woman in a season of low-slung pants—finding a pair that flatters you can be a formidable task. The solution: check-ing out the stock at vintage or consignment shops. Of course, finding exactly what you need may not be a breeze. Shopping for vintage clothes takes stamina, forethought and a real love for the hunt. But as the gorgeous vintage gowns worn by celebrities like Renée Zellweger and Nicole Kidman have shown us, the dedica-tion can be well worth it.

Renée Zellweger chose a diaphanous vintage Jean Desses gown for the 2001 Oscars.

Nicole Kidman in a vintage Loris Azzaro shirred spaghetti-strap gown at the New York premiere of *Moulin Rouge*, 2001.

GETTING THE GOODS

Shopping for vintage clothes can feel like searching for buried treasure—only there's no map. So to increase your chances of bringing home something really special, you'll have to become an expert on what different types of shops carry, what constitutes a good buy and how to assess the condition of any piece of clothing you're considering. Here's a quick primer to arm yourself for the adventure. Happy hunting!

Where to shop.

Vintage boutiques. Like a regular boutique, a vintage boutique is a well-organized store with a finely honed selection (often the owner focuses on one or two decades). The offerings are usually in great condition, often having been chosen for their collectible value, so prices can be high. The sales staff is likely to be very knowledgeable about the merchandise.

Consignment shops. People bring their high-quality, gently worn items here to make a little extra money. Generally the store owner splits the selling price with the previous owner 50-50. The proprietor will usually refuse anything that isn't clean, is in poor condition or is more than a few years old. The layout may be cluttered, but these shops are usually clean and the sales staff knowledgeable.

Thrift shops. The merchandise here has been donated, usually to benefit charity, so the inventory is huge, varied and constantly in flux. Sales help is nonexistent and the merchandise can be crammed in so tightly that pushing clothes down the rack can feel like a workout. All this means is that it takes a lot more sifting and a keener eye to find the rare amazing pieces.

Great buys.

Vintage items are often much more interesting and of a higher quality than today's pieces. So even if the price isn't exactly rock-bottom, you might be getting a bargain. Here are a few things to be on the lookout for:

Anything leather

Beaded and embellished pieces

Cashmere sweaters

Trench coats

Fur

Tailored pieces

Camel-hair coats

Cocktail and evening dresses

Julia Roberts accepted her 2000 Oscar for *Erin Brockovich* in vintage Valentino.

Finds that earn you serious bragging rights.

Classics made by the designers who made them famous are rare and incredible discoveries. Some examples:

Mary Quant minis

Yves St. Laurent tuxedos

Halston jersey dresses

Diane von Furstenberg wrap dresses (from the first time around)

Sheath dresses by Christian Dior, Coco Chanel or Hubert de Givenchy

Trench coats by Burberry or Aquascutum

Accessories made by venerable accessories houses are also a good investment. Some designers to watch for:

Gucci

Louis Vuitton

Hermès

Bonnie Cashin for Coach

Chanel

Carlos Falchi

Bottega Veneta

Develop an eye for vintage quality.

Fabric. As with all clothes—new or old—fabric is the first and best indication of quality. Find a fine fabric and you've found a fine garment. Fabric is a marriage of weave and fiber content. Since labels, if even present, usually indicate the fiber content only, you have to go by how the material feels and how it drapes. If the fabric is coarse, fuzzy or stiff, chances are the piece is not a good buy.

Condition. Carefully examine every garment for holes, stains and other signs of wear.

Hold the garment up to light to reveal moth holes or tears.

Examine seams and closures for fraying or signs of repairs. Also pull at the seams and on the fabric itself. If either feels weak, it's a sign of dry rot.

Look under the arms and examine the collar, cuffs, waistbands and closures for signs of friction or perspiration stains.

Don't buy if the fabric is shiny, faded or discolored.

With handbags, make sure all of the hardware is working.

For shoes, check for abrasions and cracks.

Label. When shopping for vintage wear, you're not looking just for big designer names. Until the mid-twentieth century, a lot of clothing was handmade—either by local dressmakers (with the label stating the maker's name and the name of the city in which she worked) or in department stores (with the tag sporting the store's name). In both cases, you're assured that the garment was not mass-produced and is of high quality. Other clues come from how the label itself is attached (completely sewn down means higher quality) and how it's made (woven labels, as opposed to printed ones, are a sign of quality).

Workmanship. Since many vintage garments were handmade, you should expect top-notch workmanship, both inside and outside the garment. Here are some tips:

One of the easiest giveaways is the buttons. If they are made of brass, pearls, bone or jet, you're in the presence of serious quality.

If the buttons aren't telling the story, then check out the buttonholes. Are they beautifully bound, or are there dangling threads?

Next, look at the seams. On the inside, have they been left raw or did the maker care enough to take the additional step of turning the edges and sewing them under or binding them? Are there bumps or ripples on the outside seams? If so, that's proof positive of a less-than-expert hand.

Always examine the lining. Is it made of a beautiful fabric, like silk, in a breathtaking color or with an interesting pattern? If there is no lining at all, that's not necessarily an indication that the garment's not high-end. If the piece is made of wool, however, it should be lined.

Surprising details like inside pockets and dress weights (metal pieces sewn into the hems to help the piece hang better) are always a good sign.

VINTAGE SIZING

Often a vintage garment has no tag indicating size, either because the label was cut out or the piece was made to measure. And even if a tag is present, the real size still remains a mystery for any number of reasons: The garment could have a European size, or it could have been altered by its previous owner. It could also have been manufactured in an earlier part of the century, when clothes were cut smaller than they are today. All of this makes it very important to try on vintage garments. Unfortunately, a dressing room is not always available in thrift shops, so regular vintage shoppers develop all sorts of tricks for figuring out if a garment will fit. Some wear baggy pieces so they can slip on pants or skirts underneath. Another idea is to just hold the garment against your body. While this will yield only a rough estimate, at least you may be able to eliminate tops without enough length in the sleeves, blouses that won't fit across your shoulders, pants that are too short, and skirts that won't accommodate your hips.

Step-by-Step Style.

Jackets.

Julianne Moore knows that perfect fit is key to a great jacket.

> The jacket is the mainstay of a woman's wardrobe.
>
> LINDA ALLARD, DESIGNER FOR ELLEN TRACY

The jacket is a wardrobe star, a piece that adds instant polish to any outfit and hides figure problems with ease. Yet for the jacket to work its magic, it must be impeccably tailored and suited to your figure. So it's particularly important to spend as much as you can afford to get a superior cut and a fabric that has just the right body. Then, look at the details: A lapel that's too wide can make you look broad; a waist that curves in too low can cut off precious leg length; and a hem that's too long can add inches to your hips.

Once you learn all the little problem areas that could be throwing off the look of your jacket, you might have a hard time finding one on the racks that meets all your requirements. Remember: It is the rare garment that wouldn't benefit from at least a nip or tuck—especially one as highly structured as a jacket. While a trip to the tailor might seem like an unnecessary extravagance of both time and money, promise yourself you'll try it once—because a well-fitting jacket is an important step toward true sartorial happiness.

Flattery.

Curvy

SHAPES:
Try a semi-fitted style that hits at the point where the hips start to curve out or that just covers the derrière.

Remember: Belted styles flatter shapely waists.

DETAILS:
Always choose single-breasted styles.

Look for a closure right below the bustline.

Keep lines simple.

Try shoulder padding to help lift the silhouette.

Narrow lapels tapered to the waist or contour seaming create a nice vertical.

Choose only flat-textured fabrics that drape well.

AVOID:
Short, rolled lapels, flapped pockets and cropped styles.

Short

SHAPE:
Look for shorter styles.

DETAILS:
Keep lines simple.

Always choose single-breasted jackets.

Opt for one- or two-button closures.

Look for jackets with narrow lapels that taper above your natural waist.

AVOID:
Long jackets, double-breasted styles and excess detailing.

Boyish

SHAPE:
Look for a fitted style that is mid-hip in length and nipped at the waist.

Belted and double-breasted styles are good options.

DETAILS:
Try heavier fabrics and textures.

Breast pockets and other details that add an extra layer of fabric will help to add shape.

AVOID:
Built-in shaping.

Narrow Shoulders

SHAPES:
Consider boxy Chanel-type jackets or double-breasted styles that flatter.

DETAILS:
Always wear shoulder pads.

A wider neck opening (a V or a sweetheart) or a military style with epaulettes give the illusion of greater breadth.

Use set-in sleeves with square shoulder pads to straighten sloping shoulders.

AVOID:
Dropped sleeves and deep armholes.

Broad Shoulders

SHAPES:
Longer styles and loose, unstructured jackets help de-emphasize the shoulder.

DETAILS:
Try deep armholes and raglan, kimono or dropped sleeves to soften shoulders.

Choose V-necks, small lapels, small narrow collars and single-breasted styles.

Elongate the torso with vertical seaming and notch or shawl collars.

If your hips are narrow, use flap or patch pockets to add weight to the hips, and balance large shoulders.

AVOID:
Anything that is fitted and/or emphasizes the shoulders, such as large lapels, short, rolled lapels or yokes; double-breasted styles; breast pockets; trims or piping; high, closed necklines and shoulder pads.

Full Bust

SHAPES:
Choose fitted or semi-fitted styles with deep V-necks.

DETAILS:
Always go for single-breasted tops.

Choose contour seaming, which can be very flattering.

Opt for narrow lapels tapered to the waist.

Look for a closure right below the bustline—anything lower, and the jacket could gape open.

Choose only flat-textured fabrics that drape well.

AVOID:
High, round necklines, double-breasted or belted styles, patch pockets, and short rolled lapels.

Small Bust

SHAPES:
Look for fitted jackets, nipped at the waist.

Consider double-breasted or belted styles.

DETAILS:
Use draping at the shoulder and down the front, breast pockets, seaming and shirring to enhance a smaller bustline.

Try shaped or scooped necklines, which are the most flattering.

AVOID:
Too much shaping at the bust.

Tummy

SHAPE:
Choose semi-fitted or straight-cut styles that reach below the derrière —or even longer.

DETAILS:
Keep all detailing vertical and narrow.

Use a deep V-neck to elongate the torso.

Opt for single-breasted closures.

AVOID:
Cropped jackets that end at the stomach, flap or patch pockets, double-breasted styles and wide collars and lapels.

Short-Waisted

SHAPE:
Look for a semi-fitted style that reaches below the derrière.

DETAILS:
Go with single-breasted styles.

Opt for one- or two-button closures, which create a deep "V" that will elongate your torso.

Use narrow lapels tapered to the waist to create a nice vertical line.

Look for a bit of shoulder padding.

AVOID:
Flap or patch pockets, wide collars, high round necklines and double-breasted styles.

Long-Waisted

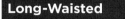

SHAPES:
Choose cropped or medium-length semi-fitted styles, and pair with a bottom that is longer in comparison (short over long).

DETAILS:
Look for a jacket that tapers in a bit above your natural waist for more leg length.

AVOID:
Very long styles.

Bottom-Heavy

SHAPES:
Try semi-fitted styles that either hit as your hips begin to curve out or just cover your derrière.

A car-coat style, worn over a sheath, will give you a long, lean line.

DETAILS:
Always choose single-breasted styles.

Add vertical details above the waist, such as shawl collars and contour seaming.

A bit of shoulder padding helps balance.

AVOID:
Short jackets, flap or patch pockets and double-breasted styles.

Fit.

Collar and Neckline

The collar should hit near the middle of the neck, without standing away from it. There should be no fabric bunching up underneath the collar in back. If a jacket doesn't have a collar, the curve of the neck opening must be in a smooth line that just grazes the collarbone in front.

Shoulders

A jacket's shoulders must sit perfectly straight and should balance on your shoulders with no drag or pull. A classic fit has the seam falling between 1/4 and 1/2 inch outside the shoulder, but flattery may dictate otherwise. Any pull across or pressure on the shoulders means that the jacket is too small. If you can't reach forward or move your arms over your head without feeling pressure in the chest, try the next size up or a different cut.

Lapels

Medium lapels, which are the classic style, are approximately two and a half inches wide. Each lapel should sit flat against the body and begin its roll just above the uppermost button. If the lapels gape, the jacket is too small in the back and chest.

Body

A jacket should fit without clinging. A fit that's too snug creates horizontal lines across the back, pulls at the hips and/or opens the back vents. In the dressing room, button the jacket and raise and lower your arms, making sure that the jacket falls back into place without needing to be readjusted. Ensure that there is enough room in the armholes for movement. Any curve at the waist of the jacket should be smooth and subtle, moving in, then out and down without flaring.

Button Closure

When your jacket is fastened, you should be able to sit down comfortably. If a jacket is too tight, an "X" pattern of pulled fabric will form over the fastened buttons.

Sleeves

When your hands hang at your sides, the sleeves should just cover your wrist bone. They should also taper toward your wrist.

Hem

When you look at the hem from the side, it should be straight all around, with no dipping in the front or back.

How a tailor can help.

Tips from Joseph Ting of Dynasty Tailors in New York:

Lapels can be cut down and reshaped.

A jacket can be changed from a three-button closure to a two-button one. (Refolding the lapel makes it longer and lower and hides the top buttonhole).

A jacket can be changed from double-breasted to single-breasted. This is a major alteration, usually costing about $200. (The tailor must take apart the entire front and re-cut it.)

Sleeves can be shortened or lengthened. (How much extra length can be added is a matter of how much fabric the maker left folded underneath, which is usually no more than two inches.)

Shoulders can be reshaped, most often by taking out padding and narrowing the suit, leaving a more natural shape. Be advised, though, that this can sometimes throw off the shape of the jacket. (Standard shoulder pads are about one inch thick.)

A jacket can be shortened, but usually no more than one and a half inches. Any more, and the pocket will be too close to the bottom of the jacket. You want at least three-quarters of an inch remaining between the bottom of the pocket and the jacket hem.

The lining can be replaced. Rayon is the best and most common fabric. Silk is beautiful but tears more easily.

Center or side vents can be easily sewn closed. (Adding a vent, however, is much more difficult and can only be done if the jacket has enough extra fabric in it to widen the body and create fabric for the fold-over along the vents.)

Wherever there are seams, they can be let out. (How much depends on the amount of fabric the maker has left in the seam—usually one to two inches of fabric per seam. Since most jackets have seams along both sides and in the center of the back, they can usually be let out by a maximum of three to five inches.)

Slit pockets cannot be moved, but they can be sewn shut so the jacket retains its shape better. Patch pockets can be removed.

Armholes can be made bigger. (The tailor removes the arms and then cuts larger holes into the body. He or she will then have to cut down further on the sleeve itself to match the new width of the armhole. This means that some length might be lost from the sleeve—but if there is enough fabric at the hem of the sleeve, the tailor can make it up.)

FLATTERING JACKET FABRICS

How fabrics will behave and wear depends both on what they are made of and how they are woven. Often, however, only the fiber content is labeled. Most jackets are made from cotton, wool, silk, rayon or blends—but you are on your own to judge the quality and suitability of the weave. If you don't recognize the fabric, ask the salesperson for help, or judge the fabric by how it feels and how nicely it hangs on your body.

Classic fabrics include menswear suiting, serge, gabardine, tropical worsted, tweed and flannel.

More luxurious jackets are cut from bouclé, silk suiting, camel hair, mohair and cashmere.

Wool crepe has a bit more drape.

Boiled wool is a nice fabric for semi-tailored styles.

High-quality coated cotton or wool blended with Lycra make comfortable jackets with a more casual look.

Katharine Hepburn in *Woman of the Year*, 1942.

Pants.

Halle Berry shows how sexy a pair of pants can be.

I like to move fast, and wearing high heels was tough, and low heels with a skirt is unattractive. So pants took over.

KATHARINE HEPBURN

Basic black pants are easy to take for granted. They're always there when you need them (except when they're at the dry cleaner); they work perfectly on almost any occasion; and they go well with almost everything in your closet. But the next time you reach for them, consider this: Until the late 1960s, wearing trousers to work or to a party was not even a consideration. Now, not only do we rarely give wearing pants a second thought, we prefer them. In designer Elie Tahari's line, for example, pants outsell skirts two to one. Pants have freed us from pantyhose, they allow us to move with much greater ease, and they're sexy. A well-fitting pair showcases a woman's finest curves, makes her legs look long and elegant, and hides secrets like spider veins and not-so-pretty knees. But, to reap these benefits, you need to shop carefully. Pants hug the body at so many crucial places that finding a pair that fits the waist, derrière, hips, and thighs just the way you want takes patience, determination and, often, a trip to the tailor.

Flattery.

Flat Derrière

SHAPE:
A tight, jean-cut style works best.

DETAILS:
Use pockets, back yokes and stitching to accent hips and derrière.

Try pants with stretch to help play up curves.

AVOID:
Overly baggy styles.

Curvy

SHAPES:
Look for: classic flat-front straight-leg trousers that sit on your natural waist.

Try flattering side- or back-zip pants.

DETAILS:
If you're tall, wear pants with a slight flare.

If you're heavy, have wide pants tapered *slightly*, so that there is width in the thighs but not the calves.

AVOID:
Cuffs and very tapered styles.

Short

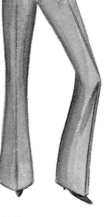

SHAPE:
Look for straight-leg trousers with front creases.

DETAILS:
Wear pants slightly long with a heel.

Match tops to bottoms for the longest look.

AVOID:
Cuffs and wide-leg pants.

Boyish

SHAPE:
Man-tailored, flat-front trousers, straight from waist to hem, should hang perfectly on you.

DETAILS:
A slight flare at the hem works for you.

If you want to create curves, try pleats or tapered pants.

Use wide waistbands and a lower rise to make your hips and bust seem curvier.

Consider hip-huggers as an option.

AVOID:
Fitted "clamdigger" styles.

Tummy

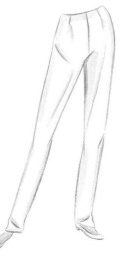

SHAPES:
Flat-front, straight-leg trousers without pockets are the shape for you.

If you have slim legs and a small derrière, consider pairing narrow side-zip or back-zip pants with a longer top.

DETAILS:
To get a loose fit at the waist, consider getting the pants' hips and behind taken in by a tailor.

Choose no waistbands or one that's an inch or less wide.

AVOID:
Belts in a contrasting color, high-waisted styles, pleats and patch pockets.

Short-Waisted

SHAPE:
A flat-front style with a slightly lower waist will give the illusion of a longer torso.

DETAILS:
So as not to shorten legs too much, wear pants slightly longer and with a small heel, to make up for the length lost above.

Wear longer tops and jackets.

AVOID:
Cropped pants, high-waisted styles and wearing the waistband of your pants on the thickest part of the stomach.

Long-Waisted

SHAPE:
Look for classic trousers that sit at or slightly above your natural waistline with straight, fairly narrow legs and no cuffs.

DETAILS:
In order to elongate your legs, wear pants slightly long, with heels and a short top or jacket.

AVOID:
Cropped pants and anything too tight.

Bottom-Heavy

SHAPE:
Look for well-tailored, flat-front trousers with wider legs that allow enough room through the hips and thighs. You may need to have the waistband taken in.

DETAILS:
A slight flare can help balance your silhouette.

The waistband should be no more than one inch wide.

If the pants fit perfectly but have side pockets, consider having them sewn up or removed.

AVOID:
Back pockets or any back detailing, wide-leg pants, bell-bottoms and all tapered, high-waisted or low-slung styles.

A SHORT HISTORY OF KHAKIS

Khakis were born in 19th-century India, when the British Army, to save its white uniforms from the swirling dust, started dying them with coffee and curry powder. The result was called "khaki," a Hindi-Urdu word for "earth-colored." In her book *Vintage Style*, Tiffany Dubin writes that this tan cotton twill fabric became the accepted tropical uniform of British and American armies and later a favorite of the privileged and preppy classes. It was Diane Keaton's rumpled and baggy pair in 1977's *Annie Hall* that propelled khakis into the fashion forefront, and a push by the Gap in the 1980s made them the versatile classic they are today.

Diane Keaton in *Annie Hall*, 1977.

Fit.

Front Creases

When you are standing straight, the crease should hang right down the middle of your leg, bisecting the knee and the shoe. If the crease falls outside of the knee, your legs will look wide.

Waistband

There should be no pulling at the closure, and the waistband should not fold in on itself when you sit. If your waistband sits below or above your natural waist, be sure that the rise is still comfortable and that pockets and pleats lie flat. (Generally, the most flattering waistline falls between an inch above or below the belly button.)

Behind (not shown)

Pants should not bag underneath or be pulled too tight across your derrière. If you must compromise, however, do so on the side of a looser fit. That way, the pants will fall straighter and give you a trimmer appearance. Avoid panty lines, which make trousers look as if they're too tight, even if they aren't.

Pockets (not shown)

Pockets of all types must lie flat and closed, and their linings should be completely invisible from the outside of the pants. It is particularly difficult for most women to wear pockets that run on a diagonal from the side seam up to the waistband. Such pockets often gape, making the hips look bigger. To keep them flat against the hips, have them sewn shut.

Rise

This is a key fit area. If the crotch hangs too low, it will cut down leg length and make you look dowdy. If it's too high, it can be excruciatingly uncomfortable and even vulgar-looking. You want a fit that is as high as possible without sacrificing comfort. Be sure to bend and sit when you try on. If there is a large fold of fabric, the crotch is too low. If you can feel it, it's too high.

Pleats (not shown)

Pleats are rarely flattering on women. Luckily, the purpose they were born to serve—providing extra room when seated—is now served by stretch fabrics. If you do wear pleats, however, be sure that they lie flat when you are standing.

Hem

When judging pant length, be sure to walk around. The hem should touch your instep in front and slope down to cover half of your heel. Try on pants with the shoes you will pair them with most often, then go 1/4 inch longer or shorter depending on other shoes you may use. In general, cuffs appear to cut off the length of your legs. But if you want to wear cuffs, they should measure about one and five-eighths of an inch in width.

Legs

Generally, pants should hang straight from the waist to the foot—unless you are wearing a tighter-fitting style, like a jean, which is meant to hug the body. As for width, a 17- to 19-inch opening at the bottom is classic, but a slight flare from the knee down is very flattering for most body types. If you're wearing tapered leg cuts, look for something subtle. If the tapering is too severe, it can emphasize your hips.

How a tailor can help.

Tips from Joseph Ting of Dynasty Tailors in New York:

The waist can be taken in or let out, depending on how much fabric is available.

Pant legs can be tapered or hemmed.

Pleats can be removed; however, this is a major alteration. (It involves cutting off the entire front panel of the pants, pulling the material flat, and then trimming the sides of the now-extra fabric and reattaching it to the sides and the waist.)

Pants can be made longer—how much longer is determined by the size of the hem, which is usually between one and a half and two inches.

The crotch can be raised or lowered; however, this is a major alteration. (To raise it, the waistband and zipper must be removed, fabric trimmed from the top, where the waist was, and the waistband and zipper replaced. Lowering the crotch is much easier.)

Widening hips and legs can usually be done by only a half-inch per side, depending on available fabric.

Linings can be added. To avoid binding at the calves, some people have pants lined only to the knee, but this can compromise the way the pants hang. Under light fabrics, a half lining can show through. Discuss it with your tailor.

Matching shoes to pants.

Straight-leg pants. For proper balance, go for a slim-soled shoe. If you wear high heels, a stiletto or princess heel with a pointed toe will make your legs look deliciously long. If you prefer lower shoes, look for a boot that isn't too clunky (with a thin sole, tapered to the toe) or a dainty tapered-toe flat. Even a loafer can work, as long as it is streamlined.

Wide-leg trousers. In order to balance out their width, wide-leg pants require shoes with a medium heel; avoid anything too high or spindly, which will make you look off-kilter. A stacked heel with a rounded toe is a safe bet. A word of caution: Make sure your pants don't fall so far over your shoes that you're in danger of tripping. If you prefer lower shoes, avoid anything too flat, or you'll appear dumpy. Wear a sandal or slip-on with a substantial sole and toe.

Cropped pants. High heels rarely work with cropped pants. Instead, stick to medium or low heel heights. If the pants hit midcalf and are tapered, a ballet or other type of flat shoe or sandal is usually appropriate. For midcalf trouser-width pants, a flat boot (as long as pants cover the tops of the boots when you sit) or something like a slim-soled loafer or small delicate-heel mule can work very well.

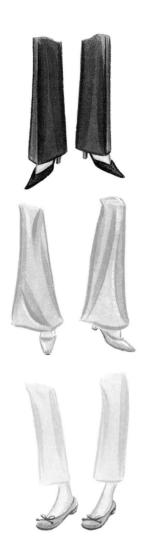

JEANS

Jeans are the epitome of American style—uncontrived, unself-conscious and oh-so-sexy—which could be why a well-worn, perfectly fitting pair is the crown jewel in many a closet. Part of their appeal is how they interact with the wearer's body, fading in all the places where the body moves. The technical reason is that the indigo dye never fully penetrates the cotton thread—it chips off little by little as the pants are worn. The resulting wear patterns are so sought after that many denim makers have come up with fascinating ways to reproduce the looks artificially (including washing jeans with skateboard wheels). And it's a good thing, because finding a pair that you'll love enough to wear for years and years can be a challenge—to put it mildly. You'll most likely have to try on a dozen or more pairs to find one that flatters your body just so—but the payoff will come every weekend, when you slip on your jeans without so much as a thought about what to wear.

Clare Danes gives her classic blue jeans a more feminine edge by pairing them with a flirty red blouse and strappy sandals.

Wearing low-slung, snug-fitting jeans, Sheryl Crow steps out in true rocker style.

Flattery.

Flat Derrière

DETAILS:
Choose stretch jeans with slim legs that hug your derrière, emphasizing the curves you've got.

Consider wearing heels to make you appear curvier.

AVOID:
Stiff denim, loose fits and boy cuts.

Curvy

DETAILS:
If you don't want skin-tight jeans, then get a straight-cut jean that is one size too large.

If you want to showcase your curves, go with a stretch jean—perhaps one with an adjustable tab in back to get a better fit at the waist. Or find a pair that fits your hips and derrière and have the tailor take in the waist.

Short

DETAILS:
Choose a classic style that doesn't overwhelm your small frame.

Look for a natural waist to add length to your legs.

Wear the legs slightly long, and pair with heels.

AVOID:
Flared or wide-leg jeans; they'll make you look shorter.

Boyish

DETAILS:
Boy cuts are perfect, so look for low-rise, straight-leg styles.

Choose a fitted behind to make you look more curvy.

Tummy

DETAILS:
Opt for styles that sit slightly lower than your natural waist.

If you have to, buy a size larger and have the hips taken in by a tailor.

Short-Waisted

DETAILS:
Look for a pair of jeans with a lower rise to elongate your torso.

Long-Waisted

DETAILS:
Wear jeans that hit near your natural waist, with straight, but not snug-fitting legs.

AVOID:
Flares, wide-leg styles, cropped cuts and anything baggy.

Bottom-Heavy

DETAILS:
Try a style with a slightly lower rise; it will allow room for the derrière without being big all over.

Consider dark denim, which better hides lumps and bumps.

Try a slight boot-cut shape to help balance out the body.

AVOID:
Tight legs or hems and small or widely spaced back pockets, which will make the derrière look bigger.

GREAT MOMENTS IN **DENIM**

The enduring sex appeal of jeans is as much due to their unpretentious styling and tough practicality as it is to their rebel mystique and body-hugging fit. Like the coolest kid in high school, they are nonchalant, completely magnetic and their popularity never wanes. Here are a few of the best blue jeans ever to appear on film:

1. Marilyn Monroe on the set of *The Misfits*, 1961.
2. Kelly McGillis and Tom Cruise in *Top Gun*, 1986.
3. Jane Fonda in *Cat Ballou*, 1965.
4. Susan Sarandon and Geena Davis in *Thelma and Louise*, 1990.
5. Thandie Newton in *Mission: Impossible 2*, 2000.

Fit.

Waist

It should sit comfortably without digging into your flesh. If your jeans are hip-huggers, be sure to sit down when trying on to make sure your backside remains covered.

Pockets

If you can see the outline of the pockets through the front of your jeans, they are too tight.

Denim Weight

Don't choose anything lighter than 12 ounces, especially if you're going to be wearing your jeans tight. (Basic Levi's are 12-14 ounces.) A lighter-weight denim will reveal bulges.

Rise

It should fit comfortably without binding. Also be careful it doesn't hang too low, which will make legs appear shorter.

Thighs and Behind

The fit in these two areas is highly personal. Some people like their jeans to hug, while others prefer them to hang straight and touch very little of the body. Neither is incorrect, just be wary of going to extremes.

Leg Width

Seventeen inches is the standard straight-leg width. It is the most classic and versatile. The slightly more flared boot cut, however, is flattering to most figures.

Hem

Jeans should fall so that there is a slight fold as the leg hits the top of your foot.

Denim glossary.

THE FABRIC

Denim. A cotton twill fabric made by weaving indigo-dyed yarn with non-dyed filling yarn.

Left-hand twill. When looking at the dark side of denim, the diagonal runs from lower right to upper left (below). When viewed on the the underside, it is the opposite. It has a softer feel than right-hand twill.

Right-hand twill. When looking at the dark side of denim, the diagonal runs from lower left to upper right (below). When viewed on the underside, it is the opposite. Traditionally used by Levi's, it is the most common twill.

Broken twill. A denim weave (below) that changes directions instead of running in a straight line.

Selvage. The tightly woven edge of vintage denim. It runs parallel to the warp and prevents unraveling.

Warp. The indigo-dyed yarn that runs parallel to the selvage.

Weft. The undyed (or filling) yarn that runs at right angles to the warp yarn.

Weight. Denim is graded by its weight per yard of fabric at a 29-inch width. Most jeans today are around 14 ounces.

DYES AND FINISHES

Enzymes. Enzymes are proteinlike substances used to eat away at the cotton fibers in denim, creating a stone-washed look.

Stonewashing. Stonewashing is a process that involves washing denim with pumice stones in order to soften and lighten the fabric (below). Chemicals or enzyme washes are often used to create the same effect.

Sandblasting. In order to age denim, makers also blast jeans with sand in localized wear areas, like the thighs, to make the jeans look worn.

Sulphur bottom. Some manufacturers apply a sulphur dye before the indigo dye to create a yellow "vintage" cast.

Yarn-dyed cloth. Yarn-dyed cloth is made from yarn that is dyed before being woven. Denim is a yarn-dyed fabric.

Garment-dyed cloth. A fabric is called garment-dyed when it has been dyed after being made into a garment. If pocket linings are also dyed, your jeans have been garment-dyed.

Whiskering. The creation of horizontal "wear lines" radiating out from the crotch is called whiskering (below). These marks used to be printed onto the jeans. Today they are created either by hand sandpapering, sandblasting or through the use of a laser.

HOW TO KEEP DENIM DARK

Turn your jeans inside out before washing. Use only cold water and add a thimbleful of vinegar. Never put them in the dryer! Also try a dye fixative, such as Indigo Fixer or Black Freeze.

Skirts.

Amanda Peet catches our eyes with a bold print skirt.

Fashion is born by small facts, trends, or even politics, never by trying to make little pleats and furbelows, by trinkets, by clothes easy to copy, or by the shortening or lengthening of a skirt.

ELSA SCHIAPARELLI

Over the years, women have adopted plenty of men's clothes as their own: the pantsuit, the tailored jacket, the constructed shirt. Still, the skirt retains a place of honor in a woman's wardrobe. It not only embraces our femininity, but there's a style out there for every facet of our personality. There's the straight skirt for feeling powerful, the flared A-line for whimsy and the pegged pencil for sex appeal. And putting on a skirt means never having to wonder if you're appropriately dressed. Although pants have become acceptable attire just about anywhere, some situations—a job interview or a wedding, for example—are better served by a skirt. But the best thing about wearing a skirt is how long and shapely it can make your legs appear. Pair a skirt in the perfect length with a little heel, and see how great you feel.

Flattery.

Curvy

SHAPES:
Subtly tapered skirts are flattering.

Consider A-lines and easy wraps as possible options.

DETAILS:
Look for flat-front styles with a side or back zipper.

If you are thick in the middle, choose dropped-waist styles or those without a waistband.

If you want to show off your waist, choose something with a waistband or belt, and tuck in your top.

Look for flat-textured fabrics with a little stretch.

Choose fabrics that are soft and fluid enough to float over your curves.

An off-center slit draws attention to the legs.

AVOID:
Boxy styles, stiff fabrics, full styles, pleats, patch pockets and horizontal detailing.

Short

SHAPES:
Try tapered straight skirts or subtle A-lines.

Make sure length hovers around the knee. Too long or too short, and the skirt can make you appear even shorter.

Consider button-front or wraparound skirts, provided they are not made of stiff fabrics.

DETAILS:
Tone top, hose and shoes to skirt.

Use an off-center slit to make legs look longer.

Try vertical detailing, such as a button-front, subtle draping, seams, trims or piping to help elongate.

Remember that a single center pleat or a hip-stitched pleated skirt will add height—but fabric must be fluid.

AVOID:
Patch pockets, hem detail, midcalf lengths and anything that is too girlish-looking (especially if you are also petite).

Boyish

SHAPES:
Go with almost any style— they're all flattering; however, if you have broad shoulders, avoid anything too full.

DETAILS:
Choose any type of pleating to flatter slim hips.

To add shape to slim hips, choose slanted pockets (those that start at the waist and go diagonally down to the side seam), gathering, patch pockets, belts and thicker waistbands.

Tummy

SHAPES:
Go with flattering, lightly tapered pencil skirts and A-line styles.

DETAILS:
Look for styles without a waistband—or have the tailor remove it.

Go for skirts with a flat front (look for side or back zippers).

Choose mostly dark colors and flat textures.

If hips and thighs are slender, consider a lighter-colored skirt, provided your tummy is covered by a darker, longer top.

AVOID:
Bias cuts, pleats (even hip-stitched), wrap styles, front darts, bulky or gathered styles and front pockets.

Short-Waisted/ Long Legs

SHAPE:
Aim for a straight shape with a dropped waist.

DETAILS:
Choose styles without a waistband.

Pair with tops that fall below the waistline.

Use styles cut from a fluid fabric to help camouflage your short waist.

AVOID:
Details or pleats that interrupt the line created by the top falling over the skirt, wide waistbands, high-waisted styles, belts of a contrasting color and any horizontal detailing near the top of the skirt.

Long-Waisted/Short Legs

SHAPE:
Straight styles will seem to elongate your legs.

Be very attuned to the right length for you. Usually it's between mid-thigh and right above the knee, or no longer than an inch and a half below. (Too long or too short will make your legs appear shorter.)

DETAILS:
Pair skirts with a short jacket or top.

Tone hose and shoes to skirt.

Use an off-center or front slit to make legs appear longer.

Try vertical detailing, such as a button front, subtle draping, seams, trims or piping, to help with balance.

Consider single pleats in front or back or hip-stitched pleats—but the fabric must be soft and fluid.

AVOID:
Horizontal patterns and any hem detail.

Bottom-Heavy

SHAPES:
Choose a moderate A-line, an easy wrap or a softly draped style.

Try tapered knee-length skirts; however, avoid anything too severe, as it will just emphasize the problem area.

DETAILS:
Opt for styles without a waistband.

Choose mostly dark and muted colors.

Look for vertical details (a center pleat or stitching) to elongate your silhouette.

Tone hose and shoes to skirts.

AVOID:
Slanted, flap or patch pockets, skirts that are pleated all the way around, bias cuts or trims, hem detail, drastic flare and horizontal details, like seams.

Fit.

Waistband

A good fit at the waist is crucial. You should be able to slip your thumb under the waistband. If the skirt has gathers near the waistband, make sure that they are not too full in any one spot, especially at the sides, which can add pounds.

Derrière (not shown)

The fabric should be taut but not tight. There should be no pulling under the waistband.

Side Seams

Seams should lie flat and hang straight from waist to hem, unless the skirt style dictates otherwise. A lined skirt usually hangs better than one that is unlined. Be vigilant about checking seams on bias-cut skirts, as they are prone to puckering.

Pleats (not shown)

All pleats must close evenly and hang perpendicular to the floor when you are standing straight.

Slits (not shown)

When you are walking, a slit should swing open and then close again when you are still, without any adjustment. A word of caution: Slits on both sides of a skirt can make you appear heavier, and front and back slits that are cut very high can be too revealing, especially when you are sitting. A safe length for a slit is no more than two inches above the knee.

Hem

When examined from the side, a hemline should hang straight, with no dipping in the front or back (unless, of course, the hemline is asymmetrical). Make sure the hem itself does not roll to the outside. The best length for your skirt is dependent on your figure (see page 65). Generally, straight, narrow skirts look better when they fall around the knee, while fuller, more fluid skirts are more flattering in longer lengths.

Mini. Minis look most fun and relaxed with flats—but not *flat* flats. Something with a little bit of lift is more flattering for most women. A small heel will work if you're trying to dress things up, but stay away from anything too high—that is, unless your legs are catwalk-worthy. In winter, the mini is a little more forgiving, because you can wear opaque tights, which help to slim your legs, and you can add knee-high boots.

Full. To offset the volume of a full skirt, you want your legs to look as long and lean as possible, so wear heels. Don't get carried away, though. Anything too high will over-emphasize your calf muscles. The shoe itself should be delicate and tapered to complement the skirt's girly vibe.

A-line. If the skirt is knee-length, a delicate, tailored shoe of almost any type will work if it has at least a slight heel. In winter, knee-high boots create a sleek look. For the warmer months, look for something that is open, like a mule. If the skirt falls at mid-calf, a lower heel or slightly heavier shoe is in order; otherwise, the skirt will overpower the shoe.

Pencil. The narrow taper of a pencil skirt makes at least a one-inch heel a necessity. Slingbacks, mules or pumps all flatter the leg and make this skirt a day-to-night staple. Since a pencil skirt is usually made from a heavier fabric, a rounded-toe shoe is fine, but a delicate pointed- or open-toe shoe, especially with a high heel, looks sexier.

Long. The longer the skirt, the more substantial the shoe should be. A small heel in a wedge or stacked style (nothing too delicate) will keep the skirt from dragging you down. In winter, long skirts also look great with boots, provided the tops of the boots are still covered when you sit. In summer, espadrilles are a classic choice. For taller women, long skirts that drape can take on a bohemian air when paired with flat sandals.

How a tailor can help.

Tips from Joseph Ting of Dynasty Tailors:

Hems and side seams can be taken up or let out. How much a hem can be let out depends on how much fabric is available. If you are shortening a straight skirt, you should talk to the tailor about having it tapered, making sure that the proportions will remain the same.

Skirts can be tapered, but they can only be widened if there is available fabric. Most straight skirts can't be tapered any more than two inches without seriously compromising your ability to walk. Bias cuts cannot be made into straight skirts.

Waistbands can be removed or let out (again, depending on available fabric).

Linings can be added or repaired.

Closures can be replaced.

Pleats and gathers can be removed.

Find your perfect length.

One thing and one thing only should determine the length of the skirt you choose: your legs. So tune out whatever is happening on the runways and forget the adages about how women of a certain age should dress. The simple rule is this: If you've got great legs, show 'em—if you don't, then don't. But figuring out whether you want "short" or "long" is only the beginning. Hem length is one place where an inch can make the difference between drop-dead and dowdy. To find the perfect length, experiment. Next time you're shopping, try on several different lengths. When you find one that makes your legs appear lean and sexy, take note of where the hem falls. It will most likely be on one of the leanest parts of your legs—usually mid-thigh or right above or below the knee. Or do your experimenting at home: Wrap yourself in a sarong and slowly pull it up until the hem hits a point that looks great. When you find that point, measure the skirt's length, or simply commit it to memory. Then continue with the experiment. Chances are, you'll be able to wear a few different lengths.

FLATTERING SKIRT FABRICS

For tailored styles. Look for mid-weight fabrics, such as wool crêpe, worsted wool, lightweight gabardine, tweed, twill, linen, brushed cotton, corduroy, denim and silk suiting.

For styles that need more drape. Wool crêpe and lightweight gabardine will still work, as will rayon, silk tweed and silk crêpe de chine.

Suits.

> Fashion is architecture: It is a matter of proportions.
>
> GABRIELLE "COCO" CHANEL

A sophisticated-looking Charlize Theron proves the power of a well-cut suit.

The suit is one of the most powerful items in your wardrobe—and, when you think about it, one of the easiest. Here is an outfit that allows you to look perfectly polished, enhances your figure and frees you from that "What am I going to wear with this?" angst. In other words, a suit can help alleviate all the stresses of dressing (appearance, self-image, comfort and ease), which is why it has remained the backbone of women's wardrobes for decades. Even in the 1980s, when all that was natural about womanly proportions was exaggerated (or simply ignored) for the sake of fashion, the suit held its own. In fact, the suit actually gained ground as workwear for women in that decade.

Today, thanks to women's rising status in the professional world, a more casual workplace and technological advancements in fabrics, the suit is more versatile, flattering and fun than ever. You can go to almost any event—a wedding, a job interview, a religious service, a party, a dinner, cocktails or even a black-tie event—in a suit. And since it is both a complete outfit and two or more separate pieces, a suit adds exponentially to your wardrobe. So when it comes time to buy a suit, carefully consider what you'll need it for, then select one that not only fills your requirements but also flatters you to great effect. Because a great suit is, without question, the wisest wardrobe investment you will ever make.

WHAT'S THE OCCASION?

How much can you really expect one little suit to do? It depends on the suit. Cut, fabric and detailing can make a suit fancy, corporate or casual—or, if you're lucky, able to shift from one look to another. The most classic suits—those with clean lines, seasonless fabrics and no flourishes—are also the most versatile: Classic suits can take you from work to an evening out with a simple change of accessories. But if you're looking for something that's appropriate for a black-tie event or weekend wear, another suit is probably in order. Here's what to look for, based on where you're going:

Work. At the office, you can't go wrong with a neutral solid or tweed fabric. Choose one that's seasonless—say, a gabardine, tropical worsted or cotton/Lycra blend—and you'll be able to wear it in all but the hottest weather. Stick to simple shapes and clean lines, avoiding anything that will date your suit or make it too distinctive, such as oversized lapels, fancy buttons, severe tailoring or any type of flourish. While pantsuits are almost universally acceptable, it's a good idea to invest in at least one skirt suit for important occasions—like meetings, presentations or a job interview.

Dinner or cocktails. Depending on how fancy the dinner or cocktail party, you can dress up your everyday work suit and look perfectly right. (See Page 69 for day-to-night dressing.) If something more formal is in order, a body-conscious cut in a slightly fancier fabric, like elegant silk or sexy leather, is better. A little bit of flourish in the form of embroidery or laser cutouts will keep you from looking "too buttoned-up."

The sporty shape of this jacket makes it great for weekend wear.

Weekend. Look for relaxed cuts—like a jean-jacket shape with a cropped pant or flirty A-line skirt in casual fabrics like denim, chino or corduroy.

Wedding. A dressy suit is a great option. A pant or skirt suit will work just as beautifully in the right fabric (something with texture or sheen, like a bouclé or jacquard). Here you can get more feminine with detailing (bracelet sleeves, for example) and colors (pastels or jewel tones).

Evening. Nothing beats the tuxedo for a little yin-yang sizzle, but there are plenty of other evening options to choose from. Look for luxurious fabrics—with lots of shine and posh or dramatic details, like a fur collar. The suit itself should be shapely to emphasize your curves and completely devoid of any sporty details, like flap or patch pockets.

A fancy brocade fabric is perfect for an evening out.

HOW TO TAKE A SUIT FROM DAY TO NIGHT

Start with a clean slate. That means a classic suit—simple lines, no details and a sophisticated fabric (wool gabardine or a matte silk)—in an inherently dressy neutral (black or winter white). Play the menswear shape of a suit against overtly feminine underpinnings that show some skin, like a silk charmeuse camisole or a lace-trimmed bustier. Or, if your jacket offers enough coverage, just button it up and forgo the top entirely. Swap your day pumps for something more delicate (an open-toe stiletto, for instance), your leather pocketbook for a small sparkly one, and your diamond studs for something big and dangly—either on your ears or around your neck. Next, doll up your hair and makeup and, voilá, you're ready to hit the town.

Night

Day

GREAT MOMENTS IN
TUXEDOS

While a man in a woman's evening dress usually looks like, well, Milton Berle, put a woman in a man's tuxedo and what you get is an electrifying sizzle. No one knew this better than Marlene Dietrich, who was one of the first women to plug into the possibilities of dressing like a man. Here are some great gender-bending moments.

1. Julie Andrews in *Victor/Victoria*, 1982.
2. Marlene Dietrich, ca. 1930s.
3. Madonna on "The Girlie Show" tour, 1993.
4. Doris Day in *Lullaby of Broadway*, 1951.

FLATTERY: THE FIRST STEP

A suit must be thought of as a whole greater than the sum of its parts. While all that you've learned about flattery and fit in the chapters on jackets, pants and skirts still applies to suit shopping, there is an added concern when it comes time to put tops and bottoms together: their proportion in relation to one another.

Fullness.

At least one piece of your outfit, top or bottom, should fit close to the body—not bodysuit-tight, but just tight enough to show some shape. Also, to enhance the straight vertical created by wearing a suit, your skirt or pants should flow seamlessly out of the jacket. What you're striving for is to have everything lie perfectly flat. The pants or skirt should not be constricted by the jacket, nor should they cause it to puff or flare out.

A flare skirt looks best with a slim-fitting jacket.

A long jacket should be worn with narrow trousers.

Length.

The goal here is to avoid cutting yourself in half visually. So think of your outfit, from shoulder to hem, as a whole. Two-thirds of that whole should be the top and one-third the bottom—or vice versa, depending on your body's proportions. To put it simply: long over short or short over long. (See page 15 for more information.) While striking this balance with all suits takes careful consideration, it is especially tricky with skirt- or dress-and-jacket suits. Pantsuits are easier to manage, because your pants will almost always be the longer part of your outfit.

Flattery.

Curvy

Play up curves by choosing fluid fabrics.

Draw attention to your waist with a shapely jacket.

Make sure that both pieces are fitted, but not tight.

Short-Waisted/Long Legs

Choose jackets with lengths that reach below the waist or farther.

De-emphasize your waistline with jackets in fluid fabrics or jacket-and-dress suits.

Elongate your torso by creating verticals above the waist.

Emphasize your leg length with narrow pants or short skirts.

Long-Waisted/Short Legs

To elongate legs, wear narrow bottoms without texture or hem detail.

De-emphasize torso with cropped jackets or high-waisted styles.

Remember that skirts are generally better than pants because they obscure the exact spot where your legs begin.

Round Middle/Thin Legs

Use vertical detailing, jacket closures and shape to lengthen your upper torso.

Find a jacket that is semifitted. It should have form, to give you curves, but it shouldn't cinch your middle.

Choose slim, simple bottoms to focus attention on your legs.

Small Top/Large Bottom

Look for details or accessories on the jacket that will focus attention upward.

Make sure to show your waistline by wearing a fitted or shorter jacket.

Enlarge the shoulders slightly to balance out your hips. Be wary not to overdo it, though, or you'll appear big all over.

Downplay your lower half with soft flowing or straight bottoms.

Large Top/Small Bottom

Avoid padding or detail on the jacket to minimize broad shoulders.

Focus attention on your hips with narrow or cropped jackets.

Look for jackets with less structure and more drape.

Add verticals above the waist.

Emphasize long legs with slim cuts.

WHAT TO WEAR UNDER THERE

While men are pretty much limited to tailored shirts (and occasionally T-shirts or turtlenecks) under their suits, women have almost limitless options. The only constraint: Your top should be becoming to both you *and* the suit. Since collared shirts are the most difficult to pair with jackets, here are a few tips:

The collar of your shirt or blouse should complement that of your jacket. If the underpinning has a rounded collar, it will not look right sitting on your jacket's pointed one. It's always best to stick to matching shapes.

Either buy a blouse or top when you're buying the suit, or take the jacket along when you're looking for something to pair with it. This is the only way to make sure the pieces match as well as you picture in your mind's eye.

Make sure that the material of the shirt or blouse is soft enough to be tucked in without bunching and long enough to stay put when you're sitting or moving around.

The pointed collar on Vanessa Williams' shirt complements her suit's wide, angular lapels.

Ashley Judd gives her suit a subtle feminine twist by wearing it with a camisole in a lighter shade of gray.

Meg Ryan creates a more casual look by pairing a conservative suit with a cotton T-shirt.

Tips for wearing and caring for your suit.

Tip #1:
Don't be afraid to separate the pieces. You can get up to a week's worth of wear from one suit and a handful of tops. The pants will look great with a twinset or printed top, and the jacket can be worn with jeans, over a dress, or with another skirt. (To avoid looking mismatched, make sure that there is a contrast between the textures or colors of the top and bottom.)

Tip #2:
Don't confuse rumpled with dirty. Unless you're prone to spilling, a few times per season is all the cleaning your suit will need. If you clean it any more often, you'll wear it out prematurely. Instead, just air it out and give it a steam. Invest in a home steamer or take it to the dry cleaner to be steamed. (Ironing can flatten lapels, imprint outlines of the suit's inner construction on the outside and make some fabrics shiny.)

Tip #3:
Always clean the pieces together. Since dry cleaning can be harsh on fabrics, you want to make sure that matched pieces become worn at the same rate. So don't dry clean one piece more often than the others, or eventually your pieces could end up mismatched.

How a tailor can help.

It's hard enough to find one off-the-rack piece that fits you perfectly—but two? Not likely. So before you even enter a store, get comfortable with the idea of alterations. You'll need them. See the chapters on jackets, pants, skirts and dresses for specifics on what can and cannot be altered by a tailor.

Fabric.

Classic fabrics include menswear suiting, serge, gabardine, tropical worsted and flannel.

Bouclé, silk suiting, camel hair, mohair and cashmere are more feminine and luxurious.

Wool crêpe has a bit more drape.

Boiled wool is nice for semi-tailored styles.

High-quality, coated cotton or wool blended with Lycra make comfortable suits that are great for travel and have a slightly casual air.

Faille, seersucker and piqué are best for summer suits.

Heavier silks and satin make great evening looks.

Dresses.

A woman's dress should be
like a barbed-wire fence:
serving its purpose without
obstructing the view.

SOPHIA LOREN

Natalie Portman looks breezy and beautiful in a colorful summer dress.

In the not-so-distant past, a woman had a different dress for every occasion. Today, we live in a more casual but also more hectic world that demands a more versatile wardrobe. That is why we buy separates: They go from one occasion to the next and can be worked into any number of outfits with ease. This has made the dress more of a splurge than a staple, but even now there are times when only the feminine look and graceful drape of a dress will do: a special date, an anniversary, a wedding or even just a beautiful spring day. But even with all its allure and sex appeal, a dress can be an extremely practical purchase. The simple black sheath, for example, flatters almost every figure and is as suitable for the office (with a tailored jacket over it) as it is for a cocktail party. But best of all, a dress is comfortable—airy and light—making it an easy throw-on for those days when you're looking to add a bit of spring to your step.

Flattery.

Curvy

SHAPE:
Go for semifitted styles that drape over curves and show off your waistline—like wraps, shifts, A-lines and belted shirtdresses.

DETAILS:
Remember that medium-weight knits and soft, drapable fabrics will flatter your curves without over-accentuating your bust and hips.

Opt for shawl collars, crossovers, sweetheart openings, keyhole necklines, off-the-shoulder styles, or strapless necklines.

If you're thick-waisted, wear diagonals on top to emphasize your shoulders.

If you're heavy, show off your legs or cleavage. Or choose an all-over pattern, which will keep the eye from resting on just one body part in particular.

AVOID:
Anything too loose or too fitted (including styles that cinch the waist too tightly), high necklines, stiff fabrics and boxy shapes or horizontal details.

Short

SHAPE:
Look for slim silhouettes—such as a semifitted sheath, wrap, shirtdress, Empire-waist style or coat dress—always matching your proportions.

DETAILS:
Keep the dress simple so it doesn't overwhelm your frame.

Incorporate vertical details—like button closures, seams and piping.

If you want to highlight your waistline, use a tiny belt.

Try a side slit to make legs look longer.

Use a higher waistline, such as an Empire-waist style, to help make your legs appear longer.

Go with monochromatic outfits.

Try a higher neckline to give you a taller look.

Lengths should hover around the knee. Too long or short, and the dress can make you appear shorter.

Tone hose and shoes to skirt.

AVOID:
Too much embellishment and very full skirts.

Boyish

SHAPE:
Try belted styles, like shirt and wrap dresses, and those with defined waistlines.

DETAILS:
Enhance curves with bias cuts and horizontals.

Use a contrasting color at the bust to add definition.

Details at the waist and an A-line skirt make for a more feminine silhouette.

AVOID:
Voluminous styles, too much tailored shaping and stiff fabrics.

Full Bust

SHAPE:
Go with semifitted styles with open necklines.

Look for shirtdress and coatdress styles, along with modified sheaths.

Try dropped-waist styles, which can be flattering.

DETAILS:
Lengthen your neckline and draw the eye up to the face with very vertical V-necks and sweetheart necklines. Emphasize shoulders with thin straps.

Choose small lapels and collars, and keep detailing on the top to a minimum.

Use vertical seams and trimmings to elongate the torso.

Use hem detail to focus the eye downward.

Look for dresses that are darker on the top than on the bottom.

Try narrow skirts with a slight flare, to balance your bust and create movement.

Choose soft, flowing fabrics.

AVOID:
High, off-the-shoulder and boat necklines, formless A-lines and tunics, gathered sleeves, styles with wide belts or waistbands and stiff fabrics.

Small Bust

SHAPE:
Try bust-defining, Empire-waist styles.

Look for wrap, coat and A-line shapes—along with semifitted sheath, chemise and shirtdress styles

DETAILS:
A plunging V-neck can be flattering.

Try smartly placed gathers, shirring and ruching, or a contrasting fabric or trim over the bust to help create fullness.

Putting a brighter color on top will help to balance the body.

AVOID:
Voluminous shapes and anything with built-in shaping that you can't fill out.

Tummy

SHAPE:
Look for dresses that obscure the waistline, like coat dresses, semifitted or straight shifts, subtle A-lines, Empire-waist styles or a dress with a matching jacket.

Tummy (cont'd)

DETAILS:
Draw the eye away from the middle of the body to the face (with open necklines or detail around the top of the dress) or to the legs (with slits or hem detail).

Try V-necks or elongated oval necklines. If the neckline is round, it should dip below the collarbone.

Use vertical seams and draped fabrics to minimize the tummy.

Go for a monochromatic look or choose an all-over pattern to keep the eye from resting in any one place.

Consider only on-seam pockets.

Look for a slight tapering toward the hemline in straight-cut styles, to narrow the silhouette.

AVOID:
Anything that cuts at the waist or has a belt, wraps, bias cuts and dresses that are too tight, stiff, bulky or gathered.

Short-Waisted/ Long Legs

SHAPE:
Choose Empire- or dropped-waist styles or anything that obscures the natural waistline, such as a straight sheath or coatdress.

DETAILS:
Use deep V-necks to elongate your neckline.

Try vertical panels and seaming to help make your torso appear longer.

Keep details to a minimum.

AVOID:
Stiff fabrics and dresses without belts or other details at the waistline.

Long-Waisted/ Short Legs

SHAPE:
Look for Empire-waist styles, coatdresses, semifitted sheaths and A-line dresses.

Try a fitted style that curves in slightly above your natural waist to help balance your figure.

DETAILS:
Focus the eye upward with detailing on the top.

Use horizontals across the middle to make your torso appear shorter.

For a leggier look, match your hose and shoes to your dress.

Be sure the hem hits you at the most flattering place or you risk losing leg length.

AVOID:
Belted styles, stiff fabrics and anything that accentuates your natural waistline.

Bottom-Heavy

SHAPE:
Go with Empire-waist styles, or anything that is tight around the bust or waist and flares slightly.

Also consider wraps, A-lines and a matching jacket and dress.

If your top and bottom are more proportional, try a semifitted shift.

DETAILS:
Emphasize your face by showing a little skin—shoulders, cleavage or arms. Also try wearing a lighter color, or some sparkle or detail on the top half of your dress.

If you're small-shouldered try a wide, open neckline, like a boatneck.

Use horizontal detailing on the top to balance.

Go for flowing fabrics on the bottom half.

Choose dresses that have very plain bottom halves in dark colors.

Vertical draping and seaming will help elongate the body.

AVOID:
Dresses that cinch the waist, pleats or bunches of fabric gathered at the waistline, stiff fabrics and any kind of detailing near the waist, hips or derrière.

Fit.

Neckline
When you are standing, the neckline should lie flat. Sit down. If you feel pressure on the throat or pulling down the back, the dress is too small. If there is a gap at the neckline, the dress is too big.

Shoulders
Seams should lie flat down the middle of your own shoulders. If there is any tugging on the shoulders when you sit, the dress is too small.

Armholes
Armholes should close around the arms without any gaping or pressure. Stretch out your arms, and sit down to make sure that there is no digging. If the dress is sleeveless, lift your arms to make sure that your bra is not peeking out at the sides.

Chest
Stand up straight to make sure there isn't pressure pushing down on the breasts or pulling through the back. Now sit down and consider these two areas again.

Side Seams
Side seams should lie flat and run straight down to the hem without puckering. Be vigilant when examining bias-cut pieces, as they tend to pucker.

Back (not shown)
There should be no pulling or gaping. If the dress has a back zipper, make sure that there is no excess tension around it.

Slits (not shown)
When you are standing straight, a slit should lie flat and perpendicular to the floor, remaining closed after you move. Sit down, making sure that the slit doesn't show more leg than you want.

Derrière (not shown)
A dress like the one shown should hint at your form without any pulling on the seams.

Hem
Look at the hem from the sides. It must hang straight the whole way around. The hem itself should not interfere with the drape and should be invisible.

SPECIALTY DRESSES

Wrap Dresses
When you're trying on a wrap dress, it's crucial to walk around, sit down and bend over. If there is not enough overlap, one strong wind could leave you more exposed than you had planned.

Belted Dresses
The width of a dress determines how much fullness will appear above and below the belt. Although some blousing can be attractive, too much is unflattering for most body types. Look at the dress unbelted; an inch of excess fabric on each side is usually plenty.

How a tailor can help.

Tips from Joseph Ting of Dynasty Tailor in New York:

Hemlines can be lowered if there is enough fabric, but check with the tailor to see if the crease where the original hemline was can be pressed out of the fabric.

Sleeves can be removed.

If the armholes on a dress are too low, they can be tightened a little at the side seam. If the armholes need more than a little tightening, a tailor will have to lift the dress at the shoulder seams—but then the neck opening will need to be reshaped, as well.

Armholes can also be enlarged, depending of the type of dress. If the dress is simple (without much detail or tailoring at the front), it can be done. If the dress is elaborately shaped (say with draping) or has lapels or long collars, altering the armholes is probably impossible without ruining the shape of the dress.

The shape of a round neckline can be changed to a V-neck or U-neck.

If the dress has a waist seam that goes all the way around, the waistline can be moved down if there is enough fabric in the bodice. It can always be raised, but doing so will change where the skirt falls on your legs. Make sure that the length will still work for you after any alterations are done.

Pleats can be removed.

Trimming and surface details can be removed or changed.

Beaded dresses can also be altered. However, the beads may have to be removed and then sewn back on after the alteration has been done. This can be very expensive. Be sure to get an estimate before having this kind of work done.

Flattering dress fabrics.

It bears repeating: Fabrics are the key to how a garment falls around a body. This is especially true with dresses. For the most flattering look, you want a fabric that gracefully moves with you. As the great French designer Madeleine Vionnet said, "The dress must not hang on the body, but follow its lines. It must accompany its wearer, and when a woman smiles, the dress must smile with her."

A few fabric suggestions:

For less-tailored styles, choose chiffon, rayon, viscose with Lycra, jersey, cotton knit or four-ply silk.

Summer dresses work best in shirting material, broadcloth, lawn, madras, poplin and piqué.

For a tailored style, look for crêpe, gabardine, cashmere or wool suiting materials.

GREAT MOMENTS IN THE
LITTLE BLACK DRESS

The little black dress is like a hint of perfume: quiet, but alluring. Its utter chic is what has made it a staple choice for countless women, reaching back to the 1920s, when Coco Chanel (who is often credited with its invention) first revealed hers. Some of our favorite movie stars have graced the silver screen in different versions of this famous favorite:

1. Rene Russo in *The Thomas Crown Affair*, 1999.
2. Elizabeth Taylor celebrates her role in *Suddenly Last Summer*, 1959.
3. Ann Margaret, ca. 1970s.
4. Audrey Hepburn in *Breakfast at Tiffany's*, 1961.
5. Marilyn Monroe in *The Asphalt Jungle*, 1950.

EVENING DRESSES

Great cocktail and evening dresses are the stuff dreams are made of. Think of Grace Kelly in the white strapless gown and diamond necklace in *To Catch a Thief*. One can't help getting a little dreamy. These days, thanks to media coverage of Hollywood's red-carpet moments, gown-watching has become something of a national pastime. And is it any wonder? All those filmy fabrics, hand embroideries, surprising cuts, shiny beads and shimmering sequins are fascinating. But add a lovely figure to the mix, and the spectacle becomes irresistible. Even outside of Hollywood, the evening dress doesn't disappoint. Wearing a gown that moves with the body—hinting at certain parts, showcasing others—allows us to be transformed for the night into a more glamorous version of our everyday selves. So don't fritter away a formal evening in a plain frock. Turn on the glitz!

At the 2003 Oscars, Kate Hudson glowed in this champagne-colored gown by Versace.

Jennifer Lopez chose a one-shoulder Valentino dress for the 2001 Golden Globe Awards.

BLACK-TIE BASICS

More often than not, the words "black tie" on an invitation open up a can of confusion. That's because not all black-tie affairs are created equal. Time, venue, host and reason for the fête must all be taken into consideration when choosing an outfit. If, for example, it's your office party that's been deemed black tie, a backless number may prove to be an overly revealing choice. On the other hand, wearing a conservative black dress to the opening night of the ballet only ensures your place among the wallflowers.

Business black tie. For those occasions when you need to show your professional side, it is best to be cautious. Think quiet and elegant. If ever there was a moment for the little black dress, this is it. Dress up a conservative style with strappy shoes and glittering jewelry. Avoid anything overtly sexy, like plunging necklines, up-to-there slits or a super body-hugging fit. Showing your shoulders in a strapless or spaghetti-strap number is fine. The rest of the dress should be pretty staid: knee length or longer. And bring a wrap.

A little black dress made more festive with a brightly colored wrap and sexy shoes is perfect for a business function.

Social black tie. Now it's time for dress-up fun. Indulge your fantasies. Get sexy, sparkly or downright glam. Social occasions—evening weddings, charity balls, opening nights—are reasons to celebrate, and your outfit should honor them as such. This is your chance to wear the red dress with the down-to-there neckline, the slinky bias-cut gown or your princess-worthy full-skirted confection.

Creative black tie. These three words leave partygoers even more baffled. The easiest solution is to call the host and ask what he or she expects. If, for some reason, this isn't possible, then you can do one of two things: Pull out your trusty black cocktail dress, or mix things up by pairing one overtly formal element with something more "day." A leather skirt with a beaded camisole, full satin pants with a knit tank top or trousers in a menswear fabric with a silk shirt and bare high heels are all good options.

Invited to a "creative" black tie affair? Try a satiny sequined camisole paired with a leather skirt.

For social black tie occasions, make an entrance in a sexy, slitted gown.

HOW TO PUT SIZZLE IN YOUR STEP

Tip #1: Skin vs. Shape
There comes a time when every woman asks herself, "Is this too much?" If you're ever in doubt, you'll be safe following this guideline: Show skin or shape—not both.

Tip #2: Illusion
Feeling pale? Skin not as taut as you'd like? See-through fabrics like gauze, mesh, chiffon or georgette cover you, but still grab attention like bare flesh.

Tip #3: Shine
Nothing glams up an outfit like shine or sparkle—but keep in mind that reflective fabrics can make you appear larger, so wear them judiciously. Put them on places—near the face or cleavage, for example—you want to play up.

Tip #4: Practice
Wearing a gown for the first time can make you surprisingly self-conscious. If you're a long-dress neophyte, schedule some practice time before the big event. Put it on with the shoes you'll be wearing and walk around your house for a half an hour or so.

Tip #5: Spend Wisely
Eveningwear is a luxury item and is priced accordingly. But even on a budget, you can score a beautiful dress. The key is to stay away from embellishment. Low-cost versions of luxurious trims like lace or beading scream "cheap!" Plus, you'll be able to wear a simple, elegant dress for years to come.

Shirts and Blouses.

> Clothes make the man.
> Naked people have little
> or no influence in society.
>
> MARK TWAIN

Helen Hunt's blouse, with its delicate fabric and feminine shaping, is a nice contrast to man-tailored pants.

Whether it's the focal point of an outfit or just peeking out of a jacket, a great blouse can add color, pattern, texture or sex appeal to your look in no time. But, alas, tops are never as simple to buy as one might hope. Stand up straight and stay perfectly still, and a shirt may look just fine. Move your arms, however, and within seconds things can go awry: Buttons gape, shoulders bunch up around the neck or the back pulls too tightly. A shirt or blouse must fit closely enough to the body to be flattering, but have enough ease tailored into it to allow total freedom of movement. All of these things make tops more complicated than they might seem at first. (Custom-made shirts can take up to thirteen measurements.) And even though a blouse can be a relatively inexpensive way to work color and fashion trends into your wardrobe, don't let cost or newness tempt you into compromising fit. Remember: It's the details that add up to a truly chic outfit.

Flattery.

There are so many different shirt and blouse styles that it's almost impossible to specify all of the shapes that flatter specific figures. (Start with some general slimming tips, below.)

General

Collar Shape/Size	Sleeves	Armholes	Bust

Collar Shape/Size

The most flattering collar shapes are the ones that are the opposite of the shape of your face. If your face is round, for example, a short, round collar will only emphasize the fullness of your face—but a long, angular collar will add length. As for the size of your collar, it should match the size of your features; if they are delicate, for example, your collar should be smallish, too.

Sleeves

Long sleeves flatter everyone—provided the sleeves are the correct length and width for the arms. Sleeves that taper at the wrist are the most slimming. This one detail can make the whole arm appear more slender. As for width, sleeves should be as narrow as possible without being tight. Short sleeves should fall straight down from the shoulder without flaring out at the bottom.

Armholes

A high armhole is universally flattering. Larger armholes obscure the point where the torso ends and the arm begins and can make a woman look larger than she is. While women with fuller arms need the extra ease provided by larger armholes, they should find a cut that allows enough room for comfort without excess fullness.

Bust

The classic men's-style shirt is cut to hang straight and loose from the shoulder. It is not meant to accommodate a bust. To adapt this style for women who wear a C cup or larger, manufacturers add pleats or gathers from the shoulder down the front, deepen the armhole or drop the shoulder—all of which can make a large-busted woman appear top-heavy. A better option is a shirt with bust darts, which allows a woman to show off her curves. Also look for fluid fabrics or those blended with Lycra, for a more fitted, flattering style. Sleeveless blouses flatter larger busts if your arms are toned.

Curvy

DETAILS:
Look for semifitted styles that end below the belt or can be tucked in.

Try wrap styles and off-the-shoulder necklines.

Create verticals with deep V-necks, small collars or narrow lapels.

Keep flourishes to a minimum.

A natural shoulder line will make you appear leaner.

Remember that styles with bust darts fit better.

Try soft, drapable fabrics, which will hint at your curves without over-accentuating them.

AVOID:
Very thin fabrics, straight up-and-down cuts, hems that end right at the fullest part of your hips and anything oversized or too tight.

Short

DETAILS:
Try simple, fitted styles.

Use higher-waisted styles to make your legs look longer.

Opt for a natural fit at the shoulder.

Use vertical details—high armholes, princess seams, high closures or mandarin collars—to make you look taller.

Stick to fluid fabrics.

Tone tops to bottoms.

AVOID:
Stiff fabrics, horizontals of any kind and anything baggy, cropped or highly embellished.

Boyish

DETAILS:
Look for shrunken versions of men's shirts.

Consider fitted tops, Empire-waist styles or narrow V-necks.

Try flared short sleeves and tabbed sleeves.

Enhance the bust with breast pockets and shirring or gathers at the top.

Use wide collars, lapels and other horizontals to add shape to your silhouette.

Try halter tops—as long as there is no built-in shaping.

AVOID:
Raglan, dolman or kimono sleeves, stiff fabrics, anything voluminous and structured tops that you don't completely fill out.

Narrow Shoulders

DETAILS:
Try shoulder pads.

Go with set-in sleeves placed slightly outside of the shoulder.

Try puffy or gathered sleeves.

Use shoulder details that create horizontal lines—like epaulettes, yokes, breast pockets and wider V-neck openings—to create the illusion of breadth.

Try wide collars, sailor collars or peaked lapels.

Use wrap tops to create stronger shoulders.

AVOID:
Raglan, dolman, kimono or capped sleeves, gathered necklines and off-the-shoulder styles.

Broad Shoulders

DETAILS:
Look for raglan or set-in sleeves that do not extend beyond your shoulders.

Stick to dark colors.

Choose deep, narrow V–neck tops.

Keep collars and lapels narrow.

Look for cuffed sleeves.

AVOID:
Wrap-style tops, wide collars, puffy sleeves, epaulettes, shoulder pads, patch pockets, horizontal lines or color blocking at the shoulders (including yokes), shiny fabrics and square, sweetheart, one-shoulder or wide-open necklines.

Full Bust

DETAILS:
Look for tops that are fitted, with deep, vertical V-necks.

Try wraps, off-the-shoulder styles and corset shapes (tight in the body, but looser in the bust).

Go with small, vertical lapels and collars, with a bare minimum of detail.

A natural shoulder line gives a leaner appearance.

Styles with bust darts often fit better.

Use a bit of shoulder padding to elongate the torso.

Try long sleeves that flare below the elbow.

Use quiet verticals, like seams, to help elongate the torso.

AVOID:
Double-breasted or other styles with horizontal detailing, wide waistbands, short sleeves with flare, big lapels and collars, large prints or stiff fabrics, droopy shoulders or anything with a baggy fit and puffy, raglan, dolman, kimono or tabbed sleeves.

Small Bust

DETAILS:
Look for fitted tops, Empire-waist styles, halters and narrow V-necks.

Create fullness with breast pockets, gathers, ruffles, shirring and ruching—or a contrasting fabric or trim over the bustline.

If your arms are slender, try flared, short or tabbed sleeves.

Wear a top that's a brighter color than the bottom.

Try wide lapels and collars.

AVOID:
Structured tops that you don't completely fill out, raglan, dolman or kimono sleeves, stiff fabrics and anything voluminous.

Heavy Arms

DETAILS:
Look for a small puff at the shoulder, which eases the armhole and helps keep a blouse from being too tight.

Try long sleeves that flare below the elbow to balance arms.

Try shoulder pads to help elongate the torso.

AVOID:
Elastic or tabbed sleeves, short sleeves with flare, tight cuffs and sleeveless, one-shoulder, strapless or off-the-shoulder styles.

Tummy

DETAILS:
Look for semifitted shirts that don't tuck in and that fall just below the waist.

Consider Empire-waist styles.

Draw the eye away from the tummy with a low neckline—V-necks or elongated ovals are best.

Try fabrics that have body, but are not too stiff or clingy.

Add vertical detailing, such as narrow lapels and high armholes.

Match the tone of tops to bottoms.

AVOID:
Lots of flourish or detail, bias cuts and belted, cropped or very fitted styles—anything snug around the belly or with horizontal detail across the middle.

Short-Waisted

DETAILS:
Look for shirts that end below your natural waist-line.

Add verticals with high armholes, narrow V-necks, button closures, lapels and princess seams.

Use tabbed collars to elongate the torso.

Keep flourishes to a minimum.

Match the tone of tops to bottoms.

AVOID:
Anything that cinches at the waist or is cropped, waistbands and off-the-shoulder or high-waisted styles.

Long-Waisted

DETAILS:
Opt for high-waisted, off-the-shoulder or cropped styles.

Try styles that tuck in (as long as the waistband sits slightly higher than your natural waistline).

Use horizontal lines—like a yoke, wide collar or square neckline—to balance the body. If the horizontals are around the middle (in a pattern or created by embroidery or detailing, say), they can create the illusion of a higher waistline.

AVOID:
Anything too long or too fitted, long, narrow lapels and princess seams or unnecessary verticals.

Bottom-Heavy

DETAILS:
Look for semifitted tops that float over your hips and derrière or ones that end right as your hips start to curve out.

Consider Empire-waist and wrap styles.

Draw the eye up with a deep V-neck or by wearing a top that is a lighter color than the bottom.

If your shoulders are small, wider necklines or shoulder pads can help balance your figure.

AVOID:
Detailing at the shirt hem, length that stops at the waist or hits at the widest part of your hips, voluminous sleeves and any styles that are too fitted or too boxy or that cinch the waist.

TAILORING AND FABRICS FOR SHIRTS AND BLOUSES

Tips from Joseph Ting of Dynasty Tailors in New York:

A collar can be made smaller and its points reshaped.

A plain collar can be turned into a button-down.

Buttonholes can always be made larger—but not smaller.

Vertical darts can be added to make a shirt fit better.

A shirt can be shortened. This is a good idea if there is too much fabric when the shirt is tucked in.

Shoulder pads can be added or removed.

Sleeves can be shortened or tapered.

Cuffs can be made tighter or looser.

FABRICS
Silk, cotton, rayon and polyester (often blended with Lycra) are the most common shirt materials. Traditional menswear fabrics—like cotton oxford cloth, broadcloth, chambray and lawn—are well suited to semifitted shirts, as are cotton and silk poplin, cotton piqué and Thai silk. Softer fabrics—such as silk or polyester crêpe de chine, charmeuse and satin—offer a more fluid fit.

Fit.

Collar

The collar should hit about mid-neck, roll smoothly around the neck and lie flat. Collar points should rest on the shirt. The top button should close without straining.

Shoulders

The shoulder seam should bisect your shoulder. The seam that joins the yoke and the sleeve should rest right on your shoulder's end, neither falling off nor pulling the sleeve up over the arm (unless the style dictates otherwise). If you're trying on a dropped-shoulder style, the seam should hang no more than an inch or two down the arm.

Bust

Check to be sure that your bust doesn't pull the blouse forward, lift the front hem, or cause the buttons to gape open—even slightly. If there is any pulling around the bust or under the arms, the shirt is too small.

Body

There should be no pulling across the upper back, upper arms or chest. To make sure that the shirt fits comfortably, cross your arms in front of you, raise them overhead and try sitting down. Side seams should hang straight from the under-arm to the hem, without puckering or pulling.

Sleeves

Sleeves should reach the point where your thumb starts to curve away from your wrist. If the sleeve has a cuff, it should fit so that you can't remove the shirt unless you unbutton the cuff. The sleeves should be wide enough so that you can extend your arms and move freely without disturbing the fit of the body of the shirt.

Length

The choice of length is largely a matter of whether you'll be tucking in your shirt. If you are tucking it in, the shirt should be long enough so that you can sit down and raise your arms without pulling the sides out of your pants or skirt. If you're not planning to tuck in the shirt, the right length is the one that is the most flattering.

STARCH

Ever unwrap your freshly laundered cotton shirt only to find a small hole or a bit of fraying at the collar and cuffs?

Too much starch may be the culprit: It penetrates the porous cotton fibers and eats at them from the inside out. If going cold turkey on the starch isn't an option, at least give your clothes a break by washing them at home occasionally to get rid of any buildup.

GREAT MOMENTS IN
WHITE SHIRTS

Like freshly scrubbed skin, a white shirt, in and of itself, is a clean and innocent thing. But something happens when it's slipped onto a woman's body. Whether it's the more overt morning-after look of a rumpled man's shirt carelessly pulled on over underpants or a prim version tucked into a skirt and framing a curvy silhouette, this simple garment's got sizzle. Check out these less-than buttoned-up beauties.

1. Cybill Shepherd, 1971.
2. Elizabeth Taylor in *Giant*, 1956.
3. Brigitte Bardot on the set of
A Very Private Affair, 1961.
4. Annette Bening in *The American President*, 1995.

Sweaters and T-shirts.

I do not believe in God...
I believe in cashmere.

FRAN LEBOWITZ

Simple things often make the biggest impact. The T-shirt is the epitome of simplicity, yet it can be one of the sexiest garments a woman can wear because knits that fit right show off curves with a casual but confident effectiveness. T-shirts and sweaters are also two of the easiest ways to add color to an outfit.

Because they are relatively inexpensive, T-shirts allow you to integrate a wild color or a trendy look into classic outfits without concern for longevity. And the T-shirt's no-frills design makes it wardrobe gold—ready for a party, a lazy Sunday, a hot date or a board meeting.

But just because something is simple doesn't make it easy to buy. For many women, the quest for the perfect T-shirt is as ongoing as the search for the perfect shade of lipstick. Once you find one, buy as many in that style as you can afford. And remember the brand, because T-shirts look tired after a season or two.

A good sweater, on the other hand, can last forever. A turtleneck, a cardigan, a pullover V-neck—buy the right style for you and these classic shapes will become old reliables. The key is to know what to expect from different yarns and weaves. A cotton knit, for example, will lose its shape much faster than a silk one, and a loose, delicate knit will sag before a tighter one. A luxurious, well-made sweater can be costly, but a smart investment now will help you avoid disappointment later, when that great black sweater you depend on gets stretched out beyond all hope.

Uma Thurman mixes and matches the soft, fluffy texture of her twin set with the soft luster of a satin skirt.

Flattery.

Generally, your neck will look longer and thinner in an open neckline, and sleeve length can work for—or against—you. Here are the most common neck and sleeve styles, and how they will affect your appearance.

Necklines

Boatneck

If you're looking for coverage, a boatneck is a much more stylish option than a crew.

The horizontal that a boatneck creates helps to make narrow shoulders appear broader and also balances out wider hips and derrières.

If you have a heart-shaped face or a long neck, this style should be flattering.

Boatnecks can work well for both small- and large-busted women.

This is not a good option for women who have broad shoulders or short or thick necks.

Scoop

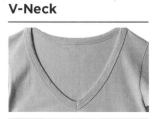

The deeper the angle of the scoop, the more flattering.

Wider scoops can flatter women with narrow shoulders or pear-shaped figures.

This neckline can make a short neck appear longer, minimize a large bust and/or balance a long, angular face.

Square

This style can balance wide hips, elongate a short neck and/or provide a counter to round shoulders.

If you have broad shoulders or a large bust, avoid this style.

V-Neck

The V-neck is a universally flattering neckline.

The deeper the diagonal of the V, the more slimming the effect.

A wider V-neck can especially flatter women with narrow shoulders or pear-shaped figures.

This neckline can elongate a short neck, make a shorter woman appear taller, balance a wide, round face or flatter both small- and large-busted women.

Crewneck

This high, round style can make the neck appear shorter; however, the effect is countered if the opening extends below the collarbone.

If you have a short neck, double chin or large bust, you should avoid crewnecks.

Turtleneck

By seeming to elongate the torso, this is another style that is almost universally flattering. However, you should probably avoid turtlenecks and cowls if you have a short neck, a round face or a double chin.

This neckline complements a long face and neck and can help shorter women appear taller.

If your neck is short or your bust large, try a lightweight knit, so as not to add bulk.

Sleeves

Long Sleeves

Long sleeves flatter everyone, but they are especially useful to women with heavy arms.

Long sleeves should fit snugly, but not tightly and should taper to the hand.

The longest, slimmest look is achieved by a high armhole, a natural shoulder, and a sleeve long enough to cover the wrist.

Half and Three-Quarter Sleeves

Both of these sleeve lengths are stylish options for heavy arms.

Half and three-quarter length sleeves present a more stylish look than most short sleeves.

Like long sleeves, these sleeves must be worn snug, but not tight. Looser versions can make your arms look short.

The armhole should be high and the shoulder natural.

Short Sleeves

This is a classic option for casual styles.

Short sleeves should fall straight from the shoulder and close to the body, without flaring.

The armhole should be high and the shoulder natural.

Cap Sleeves

Cap sleeves are difficult to wear unless your arms are thin and toned.

A correct fit is when the sleeve extends just past the end of the roundness of your shoulder.

The armhole should be high and the shoulder natural.

Sleeveless

This is a good way to deflect attention from a large bust or to show off nice shoulders or toned arms.

The arm opening should not gape or be cut so low that your bra is visible when you lift your arm.

Pay attention to where the fabric hits the shoulder and the angle at which the sleeve cuts in. If the fabric ends too far out, you will appear heavier and broader. (This is one area where an eighth of inch can make a huge difference.)

Fit.

Shoulders

Seams should be sewn flat, without puckering. Be vigilant when trying on less-expensive T-shirts and sweaters. Often the shoulder seam is not sewn down or finished on the inside—which can cause a bump in the material and irritation to the skin.

Body

For a T-shirt, the body should be snug but not tight. (You shouldn't be able to see the outline of your bra, for example.) For a sweater a close fit is generally the most flattering—but it really depends on the style and the fabric. A cardigan, for example, should hang straight and loose.

Hem

A top should end at the place that is most flattering to your figure. If you find a top you love that fits everywhere else, a tailor can easily hem it up for you. (Letting down the hem depends upon the amount of extra fabric available in the hem.) Ribbed waistbands can cause a sweater to take on a rounded shape. They should be avoided if you are curvy, bottom-heavy, large-busted, short-waisted or if you have a tummy-bulge.

T TALK

Throughout the years, our T-shirts have done a lot of talking for us. They shout political views, let everyone know we're with Stupid, prove that we're into the latest band or tell the world where we went on our last vacation. Although exactly when we started wearing our thoughts on our Ts can't be pinpointed, the first printed T-shirt on record, which reads "Dew-It with Dewey," is on display at the Smithsonian and dates back to Thomas E. Dewey's 1948 presidential campaign. Later, according to *The T-Shirt Book* by Scott Fresener, Walt Disney turned the T into the souvenir of choice. In the 1960s, the hippies spread their counterculture message —and the popularity of the T-shirt— with colorful tie-dye Ts.

FABRICS

Sweaters.

Wool. The highest quality wool is merino, which is the softest and least itchy. Also, look for pure new wool or virgin wool—both are better than reprocessed wool.

Cotton. The coolest of fabrics, cotton is great for summer sweaters. But cotton knits—especially looser ones—don't retain their shape well, so consider garments that blend cotton with spandex.

Silk. Silk sweaters are lustrous, retain their shape well and can have a gorgeous, fluid drape. Since silk is warmer than cotton but cooler than wool, it makes great transitional sweaters.

Angora. Although angora is lightweight, warm and very feminine, beware: Its fluffiness can add pounds and it sheds.

Mohair. This light fiber is stronger and warmer than wool. Although it is not as fluffy as angora, it can also make you look heavier and can be itchy.

Cashmere. Cashmere is the best sweater material you can buy. It is warmer for its weight than any other fiber, it drapes beautifully and doesn't itch. However, cashmere is very expensive. One way to cut the cost is to look for garments whose fabrics blend cashmere with wool or silk.

How a reweaver can help.

According to Ronald Moore, owner of the French-American Reweaving Company in New York:

There are two types of reweaves: the piece weave and the single-thread weave. In a piece weave, the reweaver cuts a patch of fabric from an unnoticeable place on the garment (e.g., an inner seam or cuff) and, using threads from the original garment, weaves the patch into the fabric. This can even be done on patterned fabric. The single-thread weave, which is best for smaller holes, uses only threads from the original garment to reconstruct the fabric.

If a garment is made of cashmere or wool and there is extra fabric hidden in the seams, it can be repaired by a reweaver. Even large holes can be fixed if there is enough extra material.

Cotton can be rewoven, but the result is not as good. That's because the more you work with cotton, the fluffier it becomes.

Items made of nylon, silk, acetate or rayon cannot be rewoven.

Moth holes are sometimes difficult to fix because the fabric around the hole has been weakened—so when you attempt to fix the hole, another spot often tears.

Tears, burns and stains are easier to fix because the material bordering the holes is usually in good shape.

Ribbing is difficult to fix because it has to be woven from two sides. Only very small holes on ribbed knits can be fixed.

Reweaving is expensive. A sweater with a cigarette burn is about $45. A small piece weave is usually around $95. A single-thread weave is the more expensive, starting at about $115.

BUYING QUALITY FABRIC

Cotton.
Although cotton has a lot to recommend it—it's strong enough to stand up to repeated washings and feels cool and comfortable against the skin—it lacks natural elasticity and drape. So, in the most coveted T-shirts, the highest quality cotton is blended with spandex (for better shape retention) and then subjected to finishing treatments to improve the fabric's look and feel. Mercerized cotton, for example, is stronger and more lustrous than untreated cotton, while combed cotton (which has had the impurities and shorter threads removed) has a softer feel. These additional steps add to the price of the finished product and are also what make the T-shirt you got for free from your long-distance service feel and hang so much differently from the one you bought to go under your favorite suit. Still, fabric isn't the sole reason for the higher price tag. Workmanship must be factored in, too. Details—such as a neckline that has a finished seam instead of a ribbed band, precise shoulder seams, and sleeve and shirt hems that are invisible—are more expensive to produce.

Cashmere.
Cashmere wool comes from the downy underbelly of a cashmere goat. The most valuable fibers are long and fine and usually come from Mongolia or China. Once the fibers are collected, they either stay in China or they are sent to Italy or Scotland for processing (a complex, multistep procedure that includes cleaning and spinning the fibers into yarn) and then knitted into clothing.

According to Lynn Riker of Ballantyne Cashmere in New York, whether a sweater is single or double ply (ply means thread)—or more in the case of bulky sweaters—is not the definitive indicator of quality. It depends on the quality of yarn, which is largely a function of where the sweater was made. The best pieces usually come from Europe. In general, the Italians tend to be more experimental in their treatment of the yarn and design, and the Scots stick to their centuries-old traditions.

Coats.

> My coat and I are comfortable together... [It] is complacent to all my movements. And I only feel its presence because it keeps me warm.
>
> VICTOR HUGO

Lucy Lui looks perfectly polished in this long, leather topper.

The coat is no impulse buy. Here's a garment you wear day after day. Not only do you rely on it to make a good first impression, but you expect it to protect you from the elements. And this is a huge burden—one too large for a single garment. Depending on your lifestyle and where you live, chances are you'll need a wardrobe of coats— one for everyday wear, one for rain, one for week-ends, one for evenings out, and one for the cold. Given that good outerwear can be expensive, start by focusing on the one you'll wear the most. For most people, it's a work coat. Luckily, you should be able to find one that looks suitably styl-ish both as career wear and for a Saturday night dinner-and-movie date. This coat is the ultimate cost-per-wear bargain, so snap it up.

Flattery.

Curvy

DETAILS:
First try a belted coat. Also consider a single-breasted, straight cut, or a semifitted style.

Look for simple lines and natural-looking shoulder padding.

Use narrow lapels tapered to the waist to create an illusion of height.

Enhance décolleté with soft shawl collars.

AVOID:
Flap or patch pockets, high necklines and styles that are too full or too fitted.

Short

DETAILS:
Choose a length that's no longer than an inch above the knee.

Elongate your frame with Empire-waist, high-belted or fitted styles (especially if the curve hits right above your natural waist).

Keep lines simple.

Create an illusion of height with narrow lapels tapered to the waist or a high neckline.

AVOID:
Long coats, voluminous or double-breasted styles, wide lapels and styles with excess flourish and detail.

Boyish

DETAILS:
Choose straight styles or those that are either nipped or belted at the waist.

Textured or heavier fabrics and double-breasted styles are good options.

AVOID:
Anything with built-in curves that you can't fill out and styles that are too full.

Narrow Shoulders

DETAILS:
Look for set-in sleeves with square shoulder pads to straighten round, narrow shoulders.

Horizontal detailing at the shoulders will create the illusion of breadth.

Wide necklines and lapels are flattering.

AVOID:
Dropped or raglan sleeves and unstructured styles.

Broad Shoulders

DETAILS:
Try loose, unstructured jackets. Anything too fitted will emphasize the shoulders.

Use deep armholes and raglan sleeves to de-emphasize square shoulders.

Go with a length that is mid-hip or longer.

Choose V-necks, small lapels, single-breasted styles, and narrow, small collars.

Use vertical seams and notch or shawl collars to elongate the torso.

AVOID:
Double-breasted styles, breast pockets, trimming or piping on the top, epaulettes, shoulder padding, or high, closed, round necks and horizontal lines created by large lapels or yokes or by asymmetrical closures.

Full Bust

DETAILS:
Choose a semifitted, single-breasted style with a deep V-neck.

Opt for narrow lapels tapered to the waist.

Use high armholes and a natural shoulder to create a slimmer silhouette.

AVOID:
High necklines, patch pockets, double-breasted styles and loose-fitting or belted styles.

Small Bust

DETAILS:
Look for styles with a nipped waist or a belt.

Straight, tailored cuts are also good choices.

Go with flattering details on top—such as pockets, seaming or draping at the shoulder and down the front.

Use lower necklines to draw the eye upward.

Go with high armholes to keep the style from being overpowering.

AVOID:
Drop-sleeve styles and loose-fitting styles.

Tummy

DETAILS:
Choose straight-cut, single-breasted, tailored styles. A subtle A-line can work, too.

Use a deep V-neck to elongate the torso.

Try high armholes and a natural shoulder to create a slimmer silhouette.

Go with a length that is mid-hip or longer.

AVOID:
Flap or patch pockets and double-breasted or belted styles.

Short-Waisted/ Long Legs

DETAILS:
Look for single-breasted, slim, straight styles.

Use narrow lapels tapered to the waist to create the illusion of height.

Use shoulder padding to flatter and add height to the top portion of your body.

Try these flattering lengths: at the hipbone, below the hips, three-quarters and seven-eighths.

Use high armholes and a natural shoulder to create a slimmer silhouette.

AVOID:
Flap or patch pockets, wide collars and high necklines and double-breasted or belted styles.

Long-Waisted/ Short Legs

DETAILS:
Use Empire or high-belted styles to raise your waistline.

Try very fitted coats that curve in right above your natural waistline.

Consider short coats, which can be very flattering.

AVOID:
Coats that are too long or that belt at your waist.

Bottom-Heavy

DETAILS:
Consider A-lines; loose, straight cuts or coats that flare below the waist.

Use vertical details above the waist—such as shawl collars and contour seaming—to elongate the silhouette.

Opt for a slender lapel and set-in sleeves.

Use a bit of shoulder padding to balance your shape.

Try slanted pockets to minimize wider hips.

Remember that three-quarters or seven-eighths are the best lengths.

AVOID:
Short coats that hit at your widest part, flap and patch pockets and double-breasted or narrow-belted styles.

Fit.

Collar
The collar should lie flat against the back of the neck, and the fabric should not bunch up underneath the collar.

Lapels
Lapels should lie flat against the body and begin their roll just above the uppermost closure. If the lapels gape open, the coat is too small in the back and chest.

Sleeves
Sleeves should just cover the wrist bones.

Pockets
Pockets should lie flat, without any gaping spots.

Shoulders
A coat should hang evenly and comfortably from your shoulders without feeling heavy or pulling. Reach forward and then move your arms over your head to make sure that you have a good range of motion. When you bring your arms down, the coat should settle back on your shoulders without adjustment.

Armholes
You should be able to raise your hands over your head without the coat pulling through the back.

Body
There should be no pulling anywhere in a coat. Problem areas usually include the upper back; across the tummy, hips, or derrière; and around the arms. Be sure to get a rear-view look at yourself, and take some time to sit down and move around in the coat before buying.

Closures
The front opening should hang evenly when you stand straight.

Vents (not shown)
Vents should lie flat when you are standing straight.

Lining (not shown)
The lining should not pull on the coat's fabric.

Hem
When you look at the hem from the side, it should be straight all around—no dipping in the front or back.

FIGURING FABRICS

Wool. There's a reason most winter coats are made out of wool: It holds its shape, it doesn't wrinkle easily, and it's durable, warm and slow to absorb moisture.

Cashmere. Ounce for ounce, cashmere is the warmest of the natural fibers. That means more warmth at lighter weights. Since it can be pricey and is less durable than wool, cashmere is usually blended with wool to capitalize on the strengths of both fabrics.

Mohair. Mohair is stronger than plain wool, but it tends to shed and mat when wet. Mohair and wool are often blended together to reduce cost.

Alpaca. Fabrics made with alpaca are water repellent and very warm for their weight. Alpaca (usually blended with wool) is more commonly found in lighter-weight coats.

Leather. Leather coats make great wind-breakers and, with the right lining, can be used as primary winter coats in warmer climates. Lambskin is the softest and most expensive of the leathers; cowhide and pigskin tend to be stronger but stiffer.

Synthetics. Fabrics made from polyester, nylon and microfiber resist moisture and are durable—making them great for rain-coats and active weekend wear.

What's inside. Often what's on the inside of a coat is just as important as what's on the outside. A synthetic fleece lining, while cozy and fast to dry, can be heavy. Down, on the other hand, is very lightweight—if it's good quality—and very warm. Often down is mixed with feathers, which makes the jacket less expensive, but also less warm. Look at the tag for the CUI (cubic inches) measurement, which rates down by the amount of space one ounce will take up. (The higher the CUI, the warmer the coat.) Synthetic fills (Primaloft, Polarguard) can be just as warm as down, but are cheaper and will dry faster.

Does my coat always have to cover my skirt hem?

The old edict that your coat must always be about a half-inch longer than your skirt is no longer an absolute. Today, rules are more fluid—which leaves you and your sense of proportion to figure out what looks best. While it depends on the styles of the coat and skirt, generally, you're safe if a straight skirt is longer than the coat by at least an inch. Over fuller skirts, a shorter coat should be wide or short enough not to visibly bunch the skirt fabric together.

CAMEL HAIR

Although it is softer and lighter than wool and naturally water repellent, camel hair isn't as sturdy. Camel hair and wool are often blended together to increase durability and cut cost. Check the tag; a blend of camel hair and some other fiber will be labeled as such. If a coat is made of pure camel hair, there is often a picture of a camel on the label.

BEFORE SHOPPING, ASK YOURSELF:

What's the occasion?

Everyday. Simplicity equals versatility. Choose a clean, tailored, knee-length cut in a basic color, and you'll be able to wear it with almost everything. As for fabrics, go for the lightest weight appropriate for your climate, and then layer as needed. If you live where the weather gets icy cold for at least one month of the year, invest in a separate frost-busting coat. If you're looking for something that will do double duty as a work and evening coat, choose either black or white; skip any sporty touches, like a hood or patch pockets, and add one special, but subtle, detail—like a fur collar.

Evening. For a flattering evening coat, stick to simple shapes and let the detail and fabric (a lush collar, embroidery, shine) do all the work.

Casual. A casual coat is usually shorter than an everyday coat—think car coats or peacoats—but it doesn't have to be. A coat in an active fabric, a bright color, or with sporty details ranging from waist-length to three-quarters can look great with jeans and other casual wear.

What colors are in your wardrobe?

Naturally, neutrals are the most versatile. But if your whole wardrobe is in neutral shades, then a coat in a different, classic color, like red or blue, can be a wise and stylish investment.

What will you be wearing under this coat?

If you'll be putting it on over suit jackets, make sure to try it on over a jacket.

THE ORIGIN OF THE TRENCH

Long before the first husky-voiced femme fatale turned up the collar on her trench, this coat had an important military pedigree. The trench was born at the beginning of World War I, when the British army asked Burberry to make a waterproof coat for British soldiers to wear in the trenches. The coat the company created was near genius in its utility. It was made from tightly woven gabardine, for water resistance, and cut in a full, long style that would help keep rain out of the soldiers' boots. For even more protection, the coat was given a double-breasted closure, cuff straps, a storm flap over the shoulder and a back yoke. Epaulettes and a belt with D-rings were added for carrying gear. A zip-out lining was put in for warmth and given patch pockets so it could do double duty as a bathrobe inside the tents. After the war, in a testament to the coat's practicality and great natural style, the soldiers brought them home and had them shortened for workwear. By the 1940s, this stylish coat was standard issue on the streets and had even found a key role in classic film noir.

Sophia Loren in *The Key*, 1958.

JACKETS

Looking for a jacket instead? Here's a look at a few common styles:

Jean Jackets

Curvy or Full Bust

The pockets on jean jackets make this style less flattering than other jackets. Look for a high-collared version with a snug fit and without any detailing. Avoid jackets with dropped shoulders.

Short-Waisted or with Tummy

Opt for a jacket that hits the top of the hips, with a high collar, a high armhole and a straight body.

Short in Height or Long-Waisted

Choose a snug, cropped fit.

Bottom-Heavy

You can wear the classic, straight style that hits at top of the hipbone. A snug fit will look best.

Biker

Curvy or Full Bust

Choose a high-collared version with a snug fit and no detailing.

Boyish

You can wear the classic style that hits at the top of the hipbone and has a bold, asymmetrical closure.

Short in Height or Long-Waisted

Choose a snug, cropped fit.

Bottom-Heavy, Short-Waisted or with Tummy

Opt for a jacket that hits at the top of the hips, has a high collar, a natural fit at the shoulder and a straight body.

Bomber

Curvy or Full Bust

This style will look best on you if worn open. Choose one that fits in the shoulder, is more fitted than round, and has a high neck with no detailing.

Boyish

You can wear the classic, waist-length style.

Short in Height or Long-Waisted

Opt for jackets that are waist-length or a bit shorter. Snug-fitting styles are best.

Bottom-Heavy, Short-Waisted or with Tummy

The elasticized hem of this style makes it a poor choice for your body type.

Boxy

Curvy or Full Bust

Choose a single-breasted style, with a high collar and minimal detailing. The jacket should hang at least to the hipbone and should not be oversized.

Boyish

A straight style that isn't too voluminous will look best.

Short in Height or Short Legs

This is not a flattering style for this body type.

Bottom-Heavy

A straight, single-breasted style that ends below the hips will be most flattering.

Lingerie.

Elizabeth Taylor sizzled in this lacy slip as Gloria Wondrous in 1960's *Butterfield 8*.

> Brevity is the soul of lingerie.
>
> DOROTHY PARKER

Lingerie is more than a sweet secret or a quick throw-on; it's the foundation of an outfit, capable of making clothes look better and feel more comfortable. In fact, if you neglect your lingerie needs by wearing a bra that isn't supportive or underwear that binds, even your most flattering clothes will be affected. So it's well worth learning what constitutes the right fit, how to care for your lingerie and when to replace it. Then take some time to do your shopping. Your clothes—and your comfort—depend on it.

BRAS

The brassiere can be a source of serious discomfort, but it's not bra-wearing itself that causes the trouble. According to experts, 70 percent of us are simply wearing the wrong size. Find the right bra and it will work harder for you than anything else in your wardrobe—lifting, shaping, creating cleavage or simply being seductive—all while allowing you to spend your time in comfort. So, if you're tired of racing home to free yourself from your bra's cruel grip, it's time to recheck your measurements and devote a few uninterrupted hours to trying on different shapes and styles. It may take some serious shopping time to locate your perfect match, but you'll undoubtedly find the result uplifting to your spirits as well as your body.

Find your size.

If you wore a 32B in high school, no one can take that away from you—but it just might be time to move on. Your bra size is not a static measurement. In fact, it's just the opposite: The size, shape and texture of your breasts and breast tissue change over time as you lose or gain weight, give birth, take birth control pills and age. That's why it's necessary to get refitted every six months (the average lifespan of an everyday bra)—or at least once a year. The salespeople in a lingerie boutique (or your favorite department store) will gladly help you determine your size. Many shops either have trained fitters working the floor or host special events in which fitters from different brands come into the store to offer their services. Or you can grab a tape measure and do it yourself. Here's how:

While wearing a non-padded bra, wrap a soft tape measure snugly around your ribcage, just under your bust. Add five to the measurement (if the number is even, add six), and you've got your band size (32, 34, etc.).

Next, take a loose measurement across the fullest part of your bust.

The difference between the two measurements is your cup size:
One inch=A
Two inches=B
Three inches=C
Four inches=D
Five inches=DD
Six inches=DDD

There's one last hurdle: Bra sizing is not standardized. What one maker calls a C cup could qualify as a B to another. Sometimes a 34D, 36C and 38B are practically the same cup size. All of this makes it important to remain open to trying on different styles—not only in your size, but in other sizes, as well.

BRASSIERE BEGINNINGS

Over the centuries, breasts have been propped up, pushed together and reshaped by all sorts of contraptions. Exactly when the most famous of these contrivances, the brassiere, entered the world, however, is a matter of some debate. What is known is that in 1893, Marie Tucek was awarded a patent for her "breast supporter," a style similar to the modern bra, with separate pockets for the breasts, shoulder straps and a back hook-and-eye closure.

   The first contraption to be called a brassiere didn't show up until 1913. That's when socialite Mary Phelps Jacobs was faced with the problem of what to wear under her sheer evening gown, since the whale-bone corsets that were de rigueur at the time were visible through the dress. She and her maid solved the problem with two silk handkerchiefs and a bit of ribbon, creating what would become the first widely used brassiere. Family and friends immediately began placing orders with Jacobs. On November 3, 1914, she patented her design for the "backless brassiere." She later sold the patent for $1,500 to the Warner Brothers Corset Company in Bridgeport, Connecticut.

Fit.

Cups

Your breasts should fill the cups completely, without spilling out over the top of the bra or under your arms. Wrinkly fabric in the cups means that the bra is too large or that it is the wrong shape for you. You can either go down a size or try another style with less coverage. Spillage means you need a larger cup size or a brassiere that offers more coverage. If your breasts are two different sizes, look for a bra in a stretchy fabric that fits the large breast, and adjust the straps accordingly. If the size discrepancy is great, add a fiberfill push-up pad to the smaller side.

Straps

Bra straps should sit straight and flat, without digging in or sliding. For optimal fit, straps should be readjusted after each wearing. Sliding straps may be remedied by a simple readjustment. If that doesn't work, you may want to try a racerback style. (If slippage is a problem, stay away from "demi" styles, which have straps that are set more widely apart.) Straps that pinch are a sign that you need a more supportive bra—perhaps one with padding on the straps.

Closure (not shown)

Whether in front or in back, the closure must lie flat without pulling. If you're trying a bra with a back closure, use the center hooks to judge the fit. A note about front closure: It can't accommodate slight weight gain or bloating the way a back closure can—unless the back of the bra is elasticized.

Underwire

The channels that contain an underwire should fully enclose the breast and lie flat against the chest; they should never sit on top of the breast tissue itself. Cushioning is very important. If the brassiere is not comfortable in the dressing room, it will be excruciating after a full day of wear.

Band

To anchor a brassiere properly, the band, when fastened, must make a perfect circle around your rib cage. The band should be snug—but not so snug that you can't fit a finger underneath. A bra is too large if its band is riding up your back, too small if it pushes out rolls of flesh above and below the side wings. (Remember: Since cup size changes with band size, if you need to go down a band size then you may also have to go up a cup size, or vice versa.)

Center Front

The fabric or closure should sit flat against your chest.

WHAT DO I WEAR UNDER THERE?

Problem: Visible straps.

Solution: Clear bra straps, which can be attached to any bra that comes with removable straps. They are great to wear under camisole tops and spaghetti strap styles. Look for those with hooks that match your bra's color.

Problem: What to do if you're between band sizes.

Solution: Look for a band insert. This is a fabric strip equipped with bra hooks that attaches to your bra's own hooks, thereby adding inches to the band. They come in one-hook to four-hook widths.

Problem: What to wear under sheer or backless clothing.

Solution 1: Go for an adhesive bra. There are a number of styles from which to choose, including seamless silicone bra cups, demi styles and those with push up pads or underwire. While the support they offer is less than regular bras, and the feel takes some getting use to, they do hold the breast in place, provide shaping and cover the nipples. These are not recommended for those with sensitive skin or women who wear a D cup or larger.

Solution 2: For low-backed tops, try a bra converter, which is basically a long strap that attaches to your bra's hooks and then wraps around the body. It pulls the straps downward and then makes up for lost support by anchoring lower on the torso.

Problem: How to avoid nipple show-through.

Solution: Adhesive-backed nipple covers. Applied directly over nipples, these fabric disks offer a smooth look. Great to wear with sheer or nonpadded bras, or if you're wearing no bra at all. People with sensitive skin should use with caution.

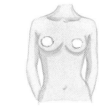

Problem: What to do about falling straps.

Solution: Look for an attachment that attaches to your bra's own straps, perpendicularly, in back. Adjust so it pulls them in toward one another. This attachment is also great for wearing with sleeveless styles and racer-back tanks.

Problem: What to do about digging straps.

Solution: Look for foam pad attachments. They slip under the bra strap and snap around it. Opt for those with tapered edges so they lie flat against the shoulder.

Problem: What to wear under a plunging neckline.

Solution: A double sticky adhesive bra. The product is actually in two pieces, one for each breast. It covers the nipples and lifts the breast, depending on placement. (Imagine you are using tape. If you anchor one side under the breast and then lift, anchoring the other side higher on the chest, you'll get some lift.) And because it is adhesive on its face, too, it allows you to fix your clothes in place so you can wear low-cut looks with confidence.

Brassiere glossary.

Convertible. A bra with removable straps that can be worn in different ways—as a conventional bra (1), a halter (2), in a criss-cross across the back or over one shoulder (3) or as a strapless (4).

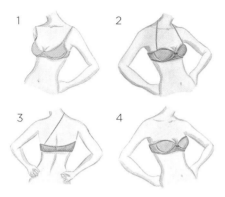

Cookie. A removable padded insert made of fiberfill or filled with water, oil or gel. Cookies are used to change the shape of the breast, as a push-up bra does.

Demi-bra. A low-cut style that just covers the nipples, leaving the top half of the breast exposed. The straps on this style are set more widely than normal. Demi-bras are meant to be worn with low or wide necklines.

Foam cup. A cup that is padded with foam to give a smooth silhouette and prevent nipples from showing through.

Front closure. A bra that closes in the center front—a good style to wear with V-necks.

Halter. A bra with straps (often removable) that fasten behind the neck.

Lined cup. A cup that offers additional support and keeps nipples from showing through.

Longline. A style that reaches to the waist and offers shaping for the upper torso. For large-busted women who can't get the support they need from a regular strapless, a strapless longline bra is a good option.

Minimizer. A bra designed to reduce projection by 1.5 to 1.75 inches by redistributing the breast. Ill-fitting minimizers can create a "uni-boob" effect—so be especially careful in the fitting room.

Molded-cup. A sculpted, seamless bra cup that provides smoothness and definition and prevents the nipples from showing through. Molded-cup bras are ideal for wearing under T-shirts and other tight-fitting garments.

Padded. A bra with a fiberfill-padded cup that makes breasts appear larger.

Push-up. A bra with padding at the bottom outside portion of the cup. These bras lift the breasts up and/or push them together to create cleavage and more definition.

Racerback. A bra with straps that make a "V" shape between the shoulder blades—good for sleeveless styles, as well as for women who have problems with strap slippage.

Seamed. Any bra that has seams running through the cup. The seams are meant to define and shape. If they run straight across the cup horizontally, they create a pointed silhouette. If they are diagonal, the bra gives a more rounded, natural look.

Seamless. Cups that are made without seams give a smoother look that is great for wearing under T-shirts and other tight-fitting clothing.

Shelf bra. Similar to a demi-bra, only slightly less coverage.

Soft-cup. A bra without structure, underwire, padding or molded cups. Soft-cup bras are very comfortable, but offer little support—making them a poor choice for women with full breasts.

Strapless. An underwire style with wide sides and no straps. The inside edges of the bra are often lined with silicone, which adheres to the skin and helps keep the bra from slipping.

Underwire. A bra with a flexible wire sewn under the bottom of each cup. The underwire—which can be metal, a metal wire coated with plastic or molded plastic—helps lift, separate and support the breasts. Highly recommended for B cups or larger.

Wide-away. A bra with widely set shoulder straps; well suited to wide necklines.

SPORTS BRAS

The way a sports bra is made and what it is made out of are the main concerns when choosing one that's right for you. Here are the pros and cons of the two main types of sports bras—compression and encapsulations—and a run-down on fabrics.

Compression bra. The classic sports bras, securing the breasts by holding them tightly against the body. This style is best for smaller-busted women. Those who are a C cup or larger can also wear them for low-impact activities.

Constructed/encapsulation bras. More like everyday bras, made with pieces, hooks and even underwires—which means that they offer more shape and support. And, because they separate the breasts, they provide better airflow than compression bras. However, constructed bras are harder to fit.

Fabrics. Fabrics play a role in support. The more Lycra a brassiere contains, the more supportive it will be. But you should consider various fabrics also for their ability to wick away moisture. Pure cotton simply absorbs moisture; you are better served by something with an inside layer made from a moisture-managing fabric, such as CoolMax.

PANTIES

Underpants might seem like something you can just grab off the clearance table and pull on. But poorly fitting panties can spoil the look of an outfit by creating bulges and lines, and force you to duck into private spaces all day to re-adjust. Luckily, today's numerous styles and lightweight, stretchy, breathable fabrics mean a lot less undie annoyance.

Playing the liberated Jill in 1972's *Butterflies Are Free* gave Goldie Hawn's skivvies plenty of screen time.

The curvaceous Raquel Welch played one of the seven deadly sins, Lilian Lust, in 1967's *Bedazzled.*

Fit.

Body

The fit should be close to the body—but not so tight that the panties bind or dig into your skin.

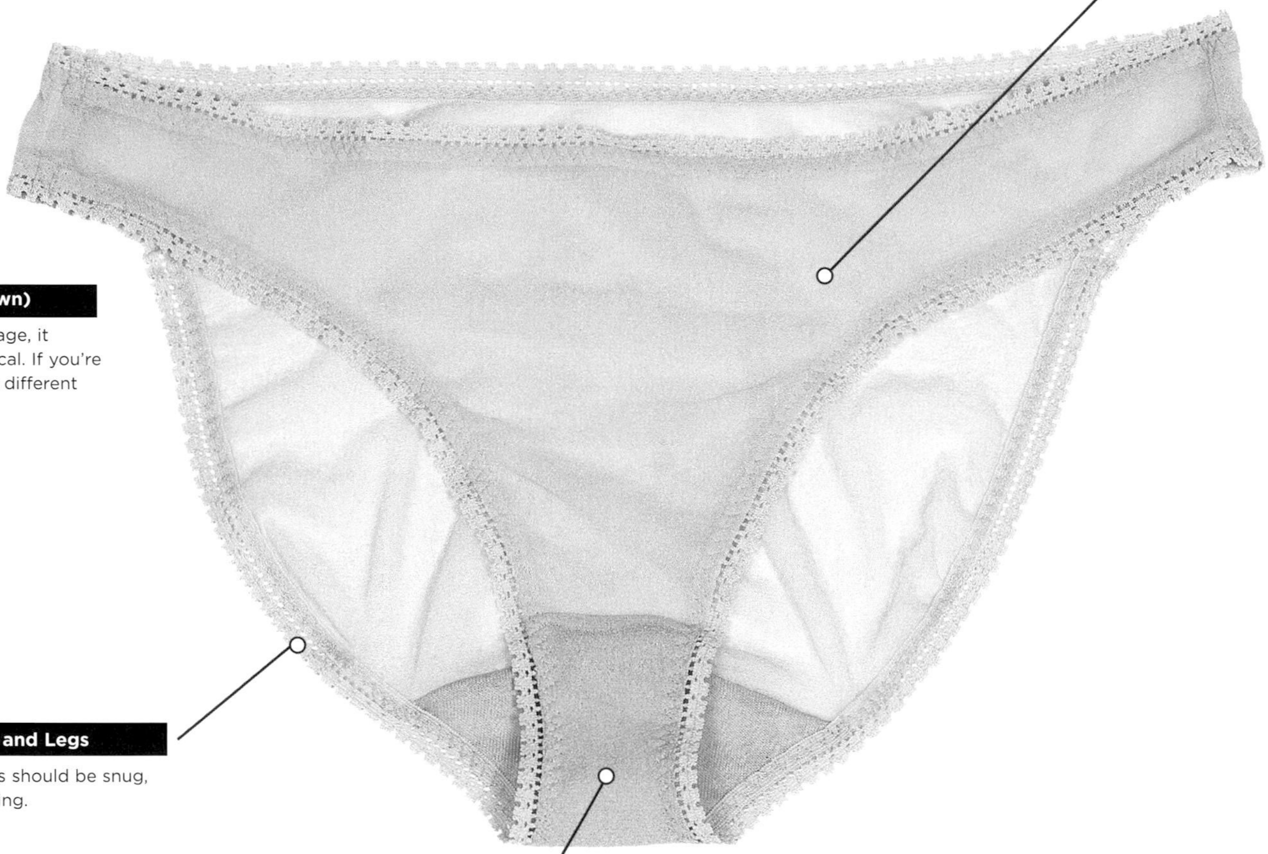

Derrière (not shown)

Whatever the coverage, it should be symmetrical. If you're tugging, you need a different size or style.

Waistband and Legs

The openings should be snug, but not binding.

Gusset

When choosing underpants to try on, examine the gusset (crotch). Are the seams smooth and flat? If not, don't even bother; they won't be comfortable. When trying on panties, the crotch should fit naturally against the body without binding or sagging. The front seam running horizontally on top of the crotch should be visible.

ERASING PANTY LINES

Here's an equation for you: Take the popularity of pants, add the advances in stretch fabrics and what do you get? An increase in thong sales, of course. While they are more popular than ever, thongs are still the most polarizing of panty styles—either you love them or you hate them. For those who are opposed, seamless, flat fabrics are the answer to a life free of visible panty lines. Even full-coverage styles will work; try a brief or a boy brief in mesh, microfiber or satin. Or look for a newer style called the "thongboy" (see page 117 for a description).

Panty glossary.

Bikini. The waistband rests below the navel and on the hips. (See also string bikini.)

Boy-leg brief. The waistline sits low on the hips, and the legs extend to the top of the thigh. Back coverage is full. This style is good to wear under short skirts and low-slung pants.

Brief. The waistband rests at or just below the navel, and back coverage is full. The legs may or may not be high cut. (See also French cut and high-cut brief.)

Control brief. A brief with added support to flatten the tummy or derrière.

French cut. High-cut legs on a brief.

G-string. Designed to prevent panty lines, this panty has no back coverage and a bikini-style waistline, and both the waistband itself and the back are made of thin strips of fabric.

High-cut brief. A brief panty with high-cut legs. (Also known as French cut.)

High-cut Rio. Similar to a string bikini, but with a more angled back.

String bikini. A bikini-style panty that has strings instead of side panels.

Tap pant. Short shorts with a slight flair at the hem.

Thong. A panty style that leaves the buttocks exposed in order to prevent visible panty lines. It offers slightly more coverage in the front than a G-string.

Thong boy. A cross between a thong and a boy brief, it offers more—but not total—coverage in the back and along the sides.

LINGERIE FABRICS AND CARE

Fabrics don't just make your lingerie look beautiful, they have everything to do with how it feels next to your skin and how well it fits your body.

Cotton. A favorite for its comfort and breathability, cotton is also durable and easy to care for. No matter what material your underpants are made from, a cotton panel is highly recommended.

Lycra. Usually blended with nylon, silk, polyester or cotton, it gives garments stretch and flexibility. This makes them more comfortable to the wearer and allows for better fit and shape retention.

Microfiber. Made from ultrafine man-made fibers, it makes for super light-weight, silky feeling undergarments that mold well to the body.

Nylon. Nylon—especially Antron® and Tactel,® both by DuPont—offers the lustrous hand and a light feel of silk only it's stronger than silk and retains shape better. Antron III® also offers static and stain resistance that make it much easier to care for.

Polyester. Strong and quick drying, polyester is an extremely popular lingerie material. Higher quality polyesters and those blended with Lycra tend to feel better next to the skin and fit the body well.

Silk. A luxury lingerie fabric that is lightweight, drapes beautifully and feels great against the skin, but it is fragile and difficult to care for.

Usually, an everyday bra lasts three to six months, and panties last about six months. Of course, this depends on how you wear and care for them. To make your unmentionables last, have more than a few in rotation and launder them carefully. Here's how:

Use a soap designed for delicates. If you machine-wash, hook your bra closed, put both bra and panties in a lingerie bag, and wash in cold water on the delicate cycle.

If you hand-wash your lingerie, which will extend its life, soak it for an hour in cold, soapy water before rinsing.

Always air dry. The heat from a dryer will cause the elastic to break down much more quickly.

Shoes and Bags.

Sexy, strappy sandals turn up the volume on Salma Hayek's outfit.

> I did *not* have three thousand pairs of shoes, I had one thousand and sixty.
>
> IMELDA MARCOS

Buying shoes and bags satisfies on a deep level because the payoff is so great. A pair of perfectly cut black pants may quietly do its part to make you look gorgeous, but a great pair of shoes or an exquisite purse positively hollers for attention and admiration. And on a practical level, many women seem to prefer shoe and bag shopping because it's just plain easier. There are fewer fit issues and almost no stripping down, which means less time in the dressing room and more showing off your new finds.

SHOES

Most of us have a tale or two that starts with us talking ourselves into buying a very cute but ill-fitting pair of shoes and ends with a Band-Aid mosaic on our heels. This is precisely the reason why it's so important to take the time to do a few extra laps around the shoe department and learn to jettison outright any pair that rubs you the wrong way. Yes, it's heartbreaking to turn your back on a great pair of shoes, but that regret is gone by the time you leave the store. The actual pain you'll feel while wearing those shoes will get you every time.

Buying the right shoes.

By willing a cute shoe to fit or convincing yourself that it will stretch out, you're not doing your feet any favors. If you shop carefully and deliberately, you'll discover great shoes that flatter and fit.

Wait until later in the day. Your feet are more swollen at the end of the day than they are first thing in the morning. You want shoes to fit your feet in their larger state.

Don't go by size alone. A size 8 in one shoe may be a 9 in another. Don't be afraid to go up or down a size. If you are lucky enough to find shoes that come in different widths, remember that width contributes to fit. For example, try the 8B versus the 8 1/2A.

Look in a full-length mirror. It's the only way to see if the proportions of the shoe complement your body. Check out your silhouette from the side and from the front.

Walk on an uncarpeted surface. Just as cushioning inside your shoes makes them more comfortable, so does cushioning outside. The only way to test how shoes will feel after you've been pounding the pavement is to try them out on a hard floor.

Move. Besides walking around, wiggle your toes, flex your ankles and sit down and stand up several times. If anything feels tight or rubs, rest assured you'll be needing Band-Aids soon.

Think ahead. Consider how you'll be wearing the shoes. If you wear an insert, you may need a larger size. The same applies to boots: Will you wear them with thick socks? If so, buy a size to accommodate that thickness; on warmer days, you can wear an insole to make up the difference.

Pairing shoes with clothes.

GENERAL

As a rule, very long and very short skirts look better with lower heels.

Narrow pants look best with lower heels.

The heavier the shoe, the more casual it becomes.

Kitten heels. These low, delicate heels are less *va-va-va-voom* than the stiletto, but they are just as flattering and even more versatile. They work well with both cocktail clothes and office attire (a suit, a sheath dress or straight, pleated and A-line skirts). Depending on the shoe, kitten heels may be paired with cropped pants.

Stacked heel. This most comfortable of high-heel styles is also the most businesslike in look, making it the perfect complement to suits and trousers.

Stiletto heel. The shoe that has launched a thousand fetishes is sexiest when paired with slim skirts. If you wear stilettos with trousers, you'll get the leggiest look by wearing the hem of your pants across the top of the shoe, allowing only the toe to peek out.

Loafer or oxford. High-vamped, slip-on or lace-up shoes look perfect with pants—think Katharine Hepburn. Only the very tall and thin should pair them with skirts.

Other flats. Flats look best with narrow and cropped pants. They also look great with long or short skirts; with a knee-length skirt, however, flats can look dowdy.

Boots. When paired with pants, boots create a seamless look. They can also be quite hip with skirts, depending on the boot's style. The easiest boot to wear with a skirt is a knee-high. Be sure that it fits snugly to the leg without digging into the flesh and that it hits above the widest part of your calf. Midcalf boots and ankle-length boots can create unflattering horizontals and are challenging to wear with skirts. You need thin legs and a sure eye to pull them off.

GREAT MOMENTS IN
BOOTS

Boots are not for the faint-of-heart. Standard issue for bikers, cowboys, cops, superheroes and those who like to dominate, they are tough, edgy and have got some serious attitude.

1. Mike Meyers and Heather Graham in *Austin Powers: The Spy Who Shagged Me*, 1999.
2. Julia Roberts and Richard Gere in *Pretty Woman*, 1990.
3. Jane Fonda in *Barbarella*, 1968.
4. Drew Barrymore, Cameron Diaz and Lucy Liu in *Charlie's Angels*, 2000.
5. Laura San Giacomo in *Sex, Lies, and Videotape*, 1989.

Flattery.

A shoe should not only feel like it fits, but look like it does. If your foot bulges over the vamp or hangs off the front, sides or back of a sandal—or doesn't quite fill it up—you need another size or style.

General

Heel

The most flattering are slim. While slim all around is best, as long as it's slim from the side, you can have some width when looking at it from the back (which will give some added support and comfort) and still achieve a leg-lengthening effect. A medium height (about two inches) flatters almost everyone.

If a heel is too high, it will not only make you feel as if you are precariously perched, but it will make your calf muscles flex—which can make your legs appear shorter.

The shape of the heel should match the shape of your body. If you're heavy, for example, a skinny stiletto will exaggerate your weight. A thicker heel style is a better option.

All shoes—even flats—are more flattering with a bit of a lift.

Vamp/Throat

The vamp, or top part of the shoe, is most flattering if cut low toward the toes. The throat, or opening, is most elongating in a "V" or "U" shape.

When worn with a skirt, a high-cut shoe (one in which less of the top of the foot shows) can make the leg appear heavier and shorter.

Wear high-cut shoes with pants.

Toe

A tapered toe gives the slimmest look. If pointed toes are too uncomfortable, look for an oval or squared-off shape. (Shopping tip: If the heels don't slip off, buy pointed-toe shoes a half to a full size larger, so your toes don't have to compete for space.)

Sole

Thin soles create the most slimming shoe. When looked at from the side, the sole should be thin—no more than an eighth of an inch thick.

Color

Usually, a shoe should be in the same color family as your outfit, but not an exact match. (When wearing black, this rule doesn't apply.)

Often, black is too heavy for a lighter-toned outfit and can cut off leg length.

White shoes are very stark and create a break in the line of your leg. Try cream or ivory. Remember, light-colored shoes make feet look bigger and show scuffs and dirt more readily.

A shoe in a vivid color, shiny fabric or with decoration can transform a basic outfit into something more exceptional. Since such shoes can also attract attention and make your feet look bigger, stick to barer styles. They are easier to wear.

Straps

T-straps, ankle straps and wide straps over the instep all cut off leg length. The effect is lessened slightly if the straps themselves are thin and more toned to your flesh. Thin straps can be uncomfortable, however.

Short Women

Very high heels can make you look off-balance. A two-inch height is safe.

If you wear flats, make sure that they have a little lift. Use the rest of your outfit to elongate, by toning shoes to stockings and skirt or to socks and trousers. Match the tone of top to bottom for even more height.

Thick Ankles/ Heavy Calves

Slingbacks are the most flattering style for you.

Boots are also a nice choice.

Always try to wear at least a half inch heel.

Shoes that are too chunky or too delicate will make your legs look heavier. Avoid square toes, stiletto heels, wedges and platforms.

Avoid ankle straps and T-straps.

Boots that hit midcalf are difficult for almost every-one, but especially so if you have thick calves, since the top of the boots will hit at the widest part of your leg.

Long Feet

Steer clear of very pointy shoes, which will make your feet seem longer. Although you still want a tapered style, look for something that is less severe, like an oval or squared toe.

To elongate the appearance of your legs, match the tone of hose to shoes. Hose should always be a lighter color.

In general, matching hose to a brightly colored shoe is too much color (red hose and red shoes, for example). Opt for flesh-colored hose.

The perfect nude is just slightly darker than your skin. Nude pantyhose should make you look slightly tan, not yellow, gray or orange.

Sheer black and gray flatter everyone. Sheers are dressier than opaque hose and should be paired with delicate shoes. Opaque hose work best with sportier clothes and shoes that have some heft.

Textured hose work best on skinny or shapely legs. One exception: A sheer, fine vertical pattern may elongate. With bias cuts, knits and jerseys, wear hose that have seamless panty tops. Don't wear hose with open-toe shoes or sandals. If a dress code demands hose, choose a translucent sandal-toe style.

The ultimate leg lengthener: A thin-soled heel with a pointed toe, V-shaped vamp and open back in a color toned to your flesh.

HIGH-HEEL COMFORT

High-heel shoes can put seven times your body weight onto the ball of your foot. But even with all of the pain (not to mention the specter of long-term trouble like bunions, backaches and twisted ankles), most women wouldn't dream of giving up high heels. After all, nothing makes the legs look longer or the strut look sexier. So how to have your heels and be comfortable, too? Choose foot-friendly shapes and flexible fabrics, and you'll be taking a step in the right direction.

HEEL HEIGHT

Problems arise mostly from heels that are over two inches high—thus, the kitten heel is a great option.

If you want to wear shoes with heels greater than two inches, do it in moderation. Wear them for only a few hours at a time, and don't wear the same pair every day—let your feet rest for at least a day.

For the most stability, a shoe's heel should be centered beneath your own.

The thicker the heel, the more comfortable the shoe. A Louis heel—which is thicker at the top and tip but thin in the middle—is an attractive compromise.

With a higher heel, a wider toe box is more forgiving.

MATERIALS

Choose shoes made of breathable materials—like napa leather or soft goat—both inside and out. Synthetics make feet sweat.

Buy shoes made of soft, flexible fabrics, like leather and suede, to allow greater freedom of movement.

A rubber or polyurethane sole is more flexible and cushioned—and, hence, more comfortable—than a leather one.

LOOK FOR STABILITY

Shoes that are secured to the feet—either pumps or those with back straps—are usually more comfortable.

Slides can make your feet work harder, and straps that are too thin can be painful.

Stay away from high-heel thongs. The strap is likely to dig in between your toes.

CUSHIONING

Feel inside the shoe for padding in the forefoot.

If padding isn't built in, buy a larger size and add an orthotic (widely available at shoe repair shops and drug stores). You can get something for the full foot—to cushion, support the arch and cradle the heel—or a simple gel pad, to cushion the front only.

HELPERS

Shoes made of leather can be stretched. (You can also try it yourself at home, using a product called Cadillac, which is sold at shoe repair shops.)

The straps and the toe box also can be stretched.

Extra cushioning can be added in the form of a very thin rubber sole, on the outside of the shoe, or a pad on the inside, under the insole.

The heel can be lowered, depending on the angle of the shoe.

Plastic heel tips can be replaced with rubber ones for a softer walk.

TIPS FROM A SHOE REPAIRER

Mike Morelli, proprietor of Brooks Shoe Service in Chicago, offers the following advice on caring for your shoes:

Take care.

Use shoe trees. They save the shape of your shoes. Newspaper is not an acceptable substitute—it absorbs the moisture in the shoe and gets moldy.

Rotate your shoes. Do not wear the same shoes every day or your perspiration will ruin them. Let them dry for at least one day before you wear them again.

Never dry damp shoes on a heater. If your shoes are soaking wet, unlace them and put them in front of a fan. If the insole is removable, take it out. When the shoes are two-thirds dry, put a tree in them and let them finish drying.

Refasten linings. If the lining of the shoe comes out, you can glue it down with rubber cement. Remove the old glue with sandpaper and dab cement on the lining. Bend up the linings' sides lengthwise and roll them in from back to front.

Add a rubber half-sole and heel tips to new shoes. These help protect shoes from wear, give you better traction and makes your shoes more comfortable. Also, both items are much cheaper to replace than an entire sole or heel. If your shoes are made of fabric, adding this extra layer to the sole is a necessity—because if the sole itself ever needs to be replaced, the fabric may rip.

Clean, protect and polish—in that order. Have whatever special cleaning products you may need, a silicone spray protector, shoe polish in neutral and basic colors, and some soft cotton or terry cloth rags—even old sweat socks—on hand. Remove loose dirt with a damp cloth. Remove salt stains with a desalting liquid, or water stains with Lincoln E-Z Cleaner (both available at shoe repair shops), following directions on the containers. Then protect all shoes, especially suede and fabric, with silicone spray. Regularly brush and lightly spray Nubuck and suede shoes and boots. Regularly polish leathers. Softer leather should be polished with a cream polish such as Meltonian Shoe Cream. Heavy leathers can take a wax polish such as Kiwi. (Wax polishes serve the same water-repelling function as silicone spray.) No matter how expensive your shoes were, they won't look it without a good polish on them. Scuffed shoes (and run-down heels) can kill your whole look.

Repairs and alterations.

Since most people's shoes wear unevenly, heel lifts need to be replaced frequently.

Heels can be raised, lowered or changed, within limits.

Straps can be added or removed, shortened or lengthened with elastic.

Closed-toe shoes can be made into open-toe shoes.

A pointy-toe shoe can be made round, but it is a difficult and expensive change.

Boot shafts can be made slimmer or shorter. They can also be made larger by adding an elastic panel.

Shoes can be dyed. Smooth leathers and fabric shoes can be tinted any color, but you'll get better results by going darker. Suede, however, is difficult to dye. If you must dye a pair of suede shoes, go within the same tone or darker.

If your shoes are stained beyond repair, have them dyed black with a penetrating dye.

BAGS

A handbag is our most trusted accessory. We take one with us virtually every place we go and rely on it to both pull together an outfit (shape and proportion are key—see page 128) *and* to stash our essentials. But a bag can go one step further: It can make your life easier. One with perfectly placed pockets can organize your stuff and eliminate any number of daily annoyances—from finding your keys in the rain to getting to your cell phone before it stops ringing. Here's how to find that precious purse.

Sela Ward's bright bag gives her all-black outfit some punch.

Selma Blair uses her bag to brighten up her graphic outfit.

How does it look?

You should always "try on" a bag and look at yourself in a full-length mirror to make sure it works with your proportions. This step may sound unnecessary, but you'd be surprised how a purse or a tote can look when you're carrying it, and how much perspective you'll gain from seeing you and your bag as other people do.

Shape. In general, your bag's shape should be the *opposite* of your body's. A structured bag is usually becoming on a round figure, while a bag with soft curves flatters a more angular one.

Proportion. Your bag should work *with* your size, not against it. A teeny bag only makes a large woman look bigger, and a huge bag is overpowering on a petite woman.

Placement. A shoulder-strap bag that hits you at your biggest part will add bulk. Women with fuller busts will find bags that hit at or below the waist more flattering. Women with wide hips, on the other hand, should look for a short shoulder bag that sits under the arm. If you're petite, you need a shorter shoulder strap—a bag that is too long can drag you down.

Color. A vivid bag is a nice way to divert attention from figure flaws.

Other considerations.

Will you be comfortable carrying it? If you'll be carrying everything from spare shoes to office files, a shoulder bag may become a pain in the neck—literally. A handheld bag, one worn across the body, or a backpack are the best options for heavy-duty carrying. Also, look at the strap itself. If it is made of a stiff material or has rough edges, it can rub you raw.

Can it handle the volume and the weight? Fill a bag with all of the things you'll be carrying. Test the weight to make sure it's not too heavy, and check to see if the bag retains its shape after it's fully loaded.

Will it keep you organized? If you've ever fumbled around in a bag looking for that lost lipstick, then you know that the right pocket placement can change your life. Do you need interior pockets for a cell phone and wallet? Would exterior pockets make it easier for you to find your car keys or work ID?

Is it secure enough for you? A bag without a top closure has more room and allows easier access—for you and for everyone around you. Check that any bag you buy has a safe compartment for your wallet and other valuables. If it doesn't, you may want to put a smaller bag inside to keep them safe.

Is it lifestyle-appropriate? Will you be commuting with this bag every day? If so, you'll need something in a hardy material, like leather or canvas.

Do you need to use both of your hands when you carry a purse, or would a hand-held bag be acceptable?

Does the strap fit over your winter coat?

Is it situation-appropriate? For example, a business bag shouldn't be made out of striped canvas, nor should you carry a structured leather bag to a baseball game.

Is it worth all that money? The quality is in the details. Check to make sure that the seams are straight and the stitching is even. Zippers and other closures should work without struggle. Edges should be finished and linings should be soft but sturdy.

PULLED TOGETHER IN A FLASH

A tried-and-true method of unifying your look is to match your shoes to your handbag. While an exact matched set can look contrived or old fashioned, pairing a bag and shoe in the same color can be truly sophisticated. Or take a cue from the set shown here, which shares stitching detail, but in reversed colors.

EVENING BAGS

Your dress, as well as the formality of an affair, dictates the style of evening bag you should choose. Here are a few pros and cons of the most common evening bag shapes:

CLUTCH

Pro: The simple design makes it versatile, complementing both cocktail clothing and more formal attire.

Con: It must be carried in your hand.

HANDBAG

Pro: Because it can dangle from the wrist, you'll be able to juggle it and a plate of food and still have a hand left over for shaking.

Con: Its structured shape keeps it from looking right at very formal affairs.

POUCH

Pro: This shape complements both formal and cocktail attire. Since you can dangle it from your wrist, it leaves your hands free.

Con: Its unstructured shape can bulge if overstuffed.

SHOULDER BAG

Pro: Great for cocktail parties, because it leaves both hands free.

Con: It's not dressy enough to be worn with formal attire, and the strap would interfere with the look of a strapless or spaghetti-strap dress.

MINAUDIÈRE

Pro: These small, hard bags work well with all evening attire.

Con: Same as the clutch—plus, the inflexible shell means no squeezing in an extra lipstick.

Tips from a bag repairer.

Chris Moore, manager of Artbag in New York, offers the following advice on cleaning and repairing bags:

CLEANING

Maintain your leather bags with a neutral polish like Meltonian Shoe Cream. First, test the cream by applying it to the bottom of the bag. If the leather discolors, do not use it.

Brush suede bags to prevent them from looking dull.

Get your everyday bag professionally cleaned by a bag repairer (or at a shoe repair shop) every six months to a year.

If your bag smells moldy, put cedar chips inside the bag for about a month.

If a pen or marker leaks in your bag, don't make it worse by using hairspray or any other oil-based product on your bag. Take it to a bag repairer. He may be able to dye your bag a darker color to hide the stain.

If cosmetics spill in or on your bag, wipe them off with a damp, clean cloth.

Don't try to clean a fabric bag at home— you may discolor it. Take it to a professional, who can spot-clean it by hand.

REPAIRS

Handles are always the first things to go. Usually, they can be replaced or repaired.

Piping around the edges can be replaced.

Scuffed corners can be dyed.

Some bags can be re-beaded. (If you notice the beads as they fall off, save them.)

Linings can be replaced.

Clasps, locks, closures and rivets can be fixed.

A tear on the gusset (side) or near the seam can be repaired, but it is expensive.

A hole can be patched.

Shoulder straps can be extended by adding chains to the bag.

Straps can be shortened.

Leather and skins can be refinished.

EMBELLISHMENT: A DELICATE BALANCE

A clutch glistening with beadwork can be mesmerizing, but before you buy an evening bag, think about your dress. Since your bag is with you most of the night, it should be in harmony with the rest of your outfit. That means striking a balance between embellished and unembellished pieces. A beaded bag is a great way to dress up a simple black dress, but an all-out sparkling gown needs a more low-key partner, like a satin or velvet bag.

Jewelry, Scarves and Belts.

Cate Blanchette dazzled at the 2000 Oscars in an antique Indian ceremonial armband among other unusual pieces.

> My mother says I didn't open my eyes for eight days after I was born, but when I did, the first thing I saw was an engagement ring. I was hooked.
>
> ELIZABETH TAYLOR

Accessories offer an easy way to create a modern, versatile wardrobe. A sparkling necklace, a silky scarf or a shiny metal belt buckle can dress an outfit up or down, take it from drab to divine, or change it from board-room professional to first-date sexy. Best of all, accessories allow you to personalize your classics. Whether you do something off-beat, like pair a conservative suit with bohemian-style earrings, or simply add a scarf in your favorite color, wearing accessories that you truly love is the most important step toward developing your own personal style.

JEWELRY

When it comes to jewelry, it's pretty darn easy to find something that strikes your fancy. Whether you're into sparkling diamonds, sleek metals or semi-precious stones, there's a color, shape and material to complement every look. And while it's a lot easier to find a pair of earrings that light up your face than to find a perfectly fitting skirt, you still need to be aware of how your jewelry will work with your features, body and wardrobe. Here's how:

The classics.

Jewelry is highly personal—no two jewelry boxes contain the same thing. But every girl should have these everyday classics, which go with everything:

Bangle bracelets. A chic set of bangles paired with a sleeveless dress or top is a summer favorite. Bangles also look great in winter when paired with a cashmere sweater.

Watch. A simple style with a neutral leather or metal band will complement both your wardrobe and the rest of your jewelry.

Stud earrings. Diamonds are the best choice because of how they light up the face. (If you can't afford the real thing, try cubic zirconia, which can be just as dazzling.) Good quality pearls can do the same thing—and you can afford bigger ones. Silver or gold studs are also practical.

Hoops or dangles. An earring with flare is great to have on hand for your more simple outfits.

A delicate necklace. An open neckline screams for adornment. A thin chain with a small pendant will go with almost anything you have.

Ready. Set. Drama.

So … you've been invited to an art opening—tonight! Thank goodness for that little black dress. But your clothes are only half of the story. You won't look completely dressed—or dressed up—without jewelry. To avoid last-minute panic, have one or two pieces of "statement" jewelry on hand—something sufficiently "glam," something you love. An easy choice is a pair of glittery earrings, like those below; it's a style that goes with virtually every neckline. A necklace is another great option—especially if you tend to wear a certain type of neckline. Or, if you want something more surprising, a pair of chunky gold cuffs can look fabulous.

Is it okay to mix metals?

Sure. However, to avoid looking like you grabbed at random from your jewelry box, use pieces that are similar in style, tone and shine. Or wear one piece to unify the look—like the watch shown here, which has been designed using both metals.

HOW MUCH IS TOO MUCH?

After adding accessories to an outfit, always look at yourself in a full-length mirror. If your jewelry seems cluttered, it's probably time to unload. Only one piece of jewelry should be a real stand-out. If you're wearing major earrings, skip the necklace. A big necklace, on the other hand, is best paired with small studs. If it's your bracelets that are bold, wear medium-size earrings and no necklace. To make everything look unified, tone your jewelry pieces to your clothes and to each other. Again, looking at the entire outfit, only one piece should really stand out. For example, if you're wearing a camel-colored sheath, try small wooden or matte-gold bangles and matte gold studs. Then you can add a shiny gold or citrine necklace to spice things up.

GREAT MOMENTS IN
JEWELRY

Jewelry may speak volumes about the wealth and status of its wearer, but the real power of jewelry lies in its ability to make a woman shine. From the glare of a multi-carat rock to the glint of a strand of pearls, jewels never fail to dazzle. Gaze at these twinkling stars:

1. Elizabeth Taylor wearing the Taylor-Burton diamond at a party given by Princess Grace of Monaco, ca. 1970.

2. Jacqueline Kennedy, ca. 1959.

3. Audrey Hepburn in *Breakfast at Tiffany's*, 1961.

4. Princess Grace of Monaco, 1956.

5. Marilyn Monroe in *Gentlemen Prefer Blondes*, 1953.

Flattery.

General

Occasion

Choose jewelry based on where you're going. For example, if you're going to work, leave the noisy bangles or huge earrings at home.

Placement

Jewelry draws the eye. A brooch, for example, may not be the best choice for a large-busted woman. But sparkling earrings will light up your face and draw the eye upward.

Size

Match your jewelry to the size of your body and features. In general, small jewelry gets lost on a large figure, while bold jewelry can overpower the petite. Likewise, a woman with strong features can handle oversize jewelry close to her face, while someone delicate should choose smaller pieces.

Shape

Repetition of a shape emphasizes it. If your face is round, round earrings will only make it appear fuller.

Clothing

The style of your jewelry should match both your outfit and any other pieces you are wearing. Completely matched sets look dated; on the other hand, wearing a sleek modern wrist cuff with vintage earrings could seem a bit off. Instead, match those cuffs with small hoops or another geometric piece.

Color

In general, cooler-toned silver, platinum and white gold tend to complement cool-toned skin, and warm-toned jewelry, like gold, is most flattering on warm-toned skin.

Necklaces

General

A necklace draws attention to the neckline and bust. The right length, size and shape can help elongate the neck, face and torso. Here are some guidelines for choosing a necklace of the right length and style for you.

Shape

Oblong styles or ones that fall in a "V" shape flatter round faces.

Heart-shaped, square and rectangular faces are flattered by oblong and round necklaces.

Pieces that lie flat are the best option for heavy women. Chunky beads accentuate size.

Necklaces cont'd

Mid-Length

A necklace whose length hits between the collarbone and the bust flatters most figures.

Oblong necklaces that hit mid-chest flatter women with short necks, full busts or round faces.

Long

Long necklaces add verticals to an outfit and flatter those women with short necks, broad shoulders or short torsos.

If you have a large bust or a protruding tummy, a long necklace will only emphasize those areas. Instead, choose a necklace that ends above the bust.

A necklace that falls between the bust and waist can make a short woman appear taller (provided she is not too busty).

Short or High

Chokers that sit on or near the collarbone are most flattering on those with long necks and angular faces.

Women with round and square faces will not generally be flattered by chokers unless they have long necks.

Short-waisted women and those with large busts should also avoid chokers.

Earrings

General

Earrings light up the face, helping to draw attention away from figure problems. Earrings can also make your neck and face look slimmer.

Your earring shape should counteract your facial shape, not repeat it.

Drop earrings can elongate the neck and face and make you look taller. However, drop styles that are too long can have the opposite effect. A safe length for dangles is just below the jaw line.

Oval Face

Anything goes with this facial shape: round, button or hoop earrings. Dangles and triangles are particularly flattering.

Rectangular Face

Round styles and hoops are best. Straight angles and elongated styles will emphasize face length.

Round Face

Avoid large, round earrings or anything chunky that sits on the lobe. Oblongs, rectangles and straight dangles are better options. Angular designs and elongated shapes can help to slim a full face.

Heart-Shaped Face

Almost any earring style will flatter—except those that come to a point. Styles that are the opposite of your face—wider at the bottom than at the top—are most becoming.

Square Face

Small, oval or oblong earrings and hoops are best. Large and chunky styles that sit on the ear can make your face look wider.

Buying and care.

Buying

Diamonds

CUT
This does not refer to the shape of the diamond, but to how skillfully it has been faceted. The cut should be symmetrical and proportional and should increase the diamond's brilliance.

COLOR
When looking at white diamonds, those most valued are colorless or nearly colorless—meaning that they have no tints of yellow or brown. There are, however, colored diamonds, known as fancy colored diamonds, which have full body color. They are highly prized.

CLARITY
This refers to any imperfections inside or on top of the diamond. Internal features, such as fractures or feathering, are called inclusions. Anything on the surface is called a blemish. The most valuable diamonds are rated flawless (no irregularity is visible under 10-power magnification).

CARAT
This is the measure of a diamond's weight. One carat equals 200 milligrams.

Pearls

SURFACE QUALITY
(Also called complexion or cleanliness.) Imperfections on the surface of a pearl, like bumps or abrasions, decrease its value. While all pearls have some blemishes, those with fewer, less-noticeable ones are the most valuable.

LUSTER
This refers to the intensity of reflection on a pearl's surface. The more intense the reflection, the more highly prized the pearl.

COLOR
Pearls come in a variety of colors—white, gray, pink, etc. But the quality "color" also refers to overtone (a translucent color overlaying the main color) and orient (which describes iridescence on or just below the pearl's surface). Not all pearls have all three color qualities.

SHAPE
Although most pearls have some imperfection of shape, the most valuable pearls are almost perfectly round. Pearls referred to as baroque are irregular in shape. Oval or teardrop-shaped pearls are called symmetrical.

SIZE
Size is the main determinant of value for pearls. In general, larger is more rare and costly.

MATCHING
Since every pearl is different, jewelry pieces containing pearls that are closely matched in all the above qualities are definitely worthy of investment.

Be sure that a pearl necklace is strung on silk with a knot between each pearl, so they don't rub against one another.

Silver

Silver is usually alloyed with copper for strength. The highest-quality silver is sterling, which is 92.5 percent pure. All sterling sold in the U.S. must be stamped either ".925" or "sterling." Some designers also stamp their pieces with hallmark symbols to indicate where the piece was made, when and by whom. (Guides to hallmarks are widely available in bookstores and on the Web.) A piece with no marking is likely made of a different metal or is silver-plated. Even a professional can't always spot the real thing; a sterling mark is your only assurance.

Gold

The karat grade of gold (not to be confused with a carat, which measures the weight of a gem) indicates the ratio of gold to another metal. Since pure gold, which is 24 karats, is too soft to make jewelry out of, it is blended with copper, platinum or silver to increase its strength.

The highest-quality pieces are 22kt (22 parts gold to two parts other metal) and 18kt (18 parts gold to six parts other metal). In the United States, 10kt gold is the lowest grade that can be legally sold. U.S. law requires that each piece be stamped with its karat grade, so that the consumer knows how much gold he or she is getting. In other countries, gold may be marked with a three-digit "fineness" number. This number indicates the percentage of gold present (14kt gold is 58.3 percent gold, so the fineness number is 583; 18kt gold is 75 percent gold, so its fineness is 750; and 22kt gold is 91.6 percent gold, or 916).

Buying (cont'd)

Platinum

Platinum is a white metal that is 35 times more rare than gold. It is one of the densest and strongest precious metals, which means it makes very secure settings for precious stones. In fact, platinum is so dense that when it scratches, the metal is simply displaced, not lost, so platinum rings don't wear away over time as heavily worn gold and silver pieces can do.

The platinum sold in the U.S. is 90 to 95 percent pure. It is most often alloyed with iridium or ruthenium, which are other precious metals in the platinum family, and this purity makes it hypo-allergenic. (Many allergic reactions to yellow or white gold are from their nickel alloy content.)

If a piece is marked Platinum, Plat, or Pt, it is 95 percent pure. There may also be a number in the stamp: 950Pt, Pt950, or 950 Plat. Pieces that are ninety percent platinum may be labeled 900Pt, Pt900 or 900Plat.

Care

Diamonds

Diamonds can chip, so remove rings before doing rough work.

A professional cleaning every six months will keep the sparkle in your jewelry. Also have the jeweler make sure the stones are secure.

Between professional cleanings, you have three options for cleaning at home.

Soak pieces in warm water and a few drops of dishwashing detergent and gently brush away dirt with an old, soft toothbrush. Rinse in a wire strainer (never over an open drain!). Pat dry with a soft, lint-free cloth. Alternatively, soak pieces for 30 minutes in a solution of six parts water to one part ammonia. Brush softly and pat dry as above. You can use an ultrasonic jewelry cleaner only if your diamond is flawless because the cleaner's vibrations can enlarge any cracks or inclusions. These machines are also too rough on semiprecious stones and even sapphires.

Pearls

Chemicals in hairspray, perfume, nail polish or ammonia will damage pearls. To avoid contact, make your pearls the last thing you put on and the first thing you take off.

After each wearing, wipe your pearls with a soft cloth to remove any skin oils or lotions.

For a more thorough cleaning, moisten a soft cloth in soapy water (use a mild soap). Ring out the cloth and wipe the pearls, first in one direction and then in the other. Rinse by wiping with a soft cloth moistened just with water.

Never clean pearls with chemicals or solvents, which will tarnish their surface.

The cord on which your pearls are strung will stretch or break down over time. To avoid an accident, have your pearls restrung every few years.

Silver

To remove tarnish, use a silver polish (available in jewelry or hardware stores). If your piece is set with gemstones, read the instructions carefully, as these cleaners can harm some stones. After polishing, rinse and dry thoroughly with a soft cloth.

Since silver is easily scratched, never rub your silver pieces with anything other than a polishing cloth or a piece of felt.

To cut down on tarnishing, keep your silver away from air and light. Wrap it in anti-tarnish paper and put it in a plastic bag in a dark place.

Gold

To keep it gleaming, rub gold with a soft chamois or clean it using the same soap-and-water method outlined in Diamonds.

Platinum

Clean your platinum pieces as you would gold jewelry.

Although platinum is very hard, it scratches like any other metal. Most people like the soft patina of use, but it can be professionally polished to a high shine.

SCARVES

While there's no denying that handling a scarf takes practice and a lot of experimentation, the benefits are well worth it. A scarf can update an outfit or make a drab one suddenly splendid. It can save a jacket or shirt that isn't the best color for you, and it can flatter your figure. But the absolutely coolest thing about a scarf is its mutability. It can be worn in hundreds of ways. A scarf can be an ascot, a tie, a neck wrap, a belt, a hip sash, a bra top, a head covering, a skirt, or a dress. But before you get carried away and try to knot yourself a new dress, start with some simple neck wraps (see instructions on page 139). You may fumble around on your first few tries, but before you know it, you'll be an expert.

Choosing a scarf.

For easiest tying, look for scarves that are soft, drapable and thin (silk, cashmere, crêpe de chine, chiffon or charmeuse). To better judge how a scarf will drape, hold it by the corner and watch how it falls; it should look fluid instead of stiff. Also, tie the ends and see if the scarf lies flat or becomes bulky. Last, check to make sure that both sides are equally beautiful, since they will both show when it's tied.

SIZE AND SHAPE GUIDELINES.

Square
15" to 24" for neck wraps.
27" to 30" for waist and head wraps.
36" to 45" for shoulder wraps, skirts or mini dress.
54" to 60" for shawls, sarongs or longer skirts and dresses.

Oblong
For mufflers and waist ties.

Scarf flattery.

When adding a scarf to your outfit, always look in a full-length mirror. It's the only way to see if the scarf is giving you the lift it should. If, instead, the scarf makes you appear top-heavy, choked, or ill-at-ease, you'll want to loosen it, go with a different tie or forego it altogether. Here are some more tips:

Avoid placing knots or patterns where they will draw the eye to your largest parts.

A scarf tied into a choker is nice with most necklines, but should be avoided if you have a short neck.

Women with short necks and large busts look best in a scarf that is toned to their top and that hangs to (or is knotted at) mid-chest.

Most women are flattered by a scarf knotted at mid-chest.

Longer scarves (but no longer than the top of the hipbone) can make a short woman look taller and a heavy woman look narrower. Longer scarves are also flattering on women with short waists or short necks.

Match the size of your scarf to your body size. For example, a small woman can get lost in a large shawl.

The smaller the scarf, the smaller the pattern should be. Save huge flowers and paisleys for big sarongs.

Choose colors that flatter your skin tone.

Neck wrap #1.

1. Fold an oblong scarf once or twice or more in half lengthwise to the desired width.

2. Put the center of the scarf over the front of your neck, wrap the two ends around the back of your neck, across one another, and then cross back to the front.

3. Tie the two ends together. (For a flatter knot, you can also loop one end through the material at your neck before tying them together.)

4. Adjust as desired.

Neck wrap #2.

1. Fold an oblong scarf lengthwise.

2. Then fold it in half in the other direction.

3. Drape the doubled scarf around your neck.

4. Pull the ends through the loop and adjust as desired.

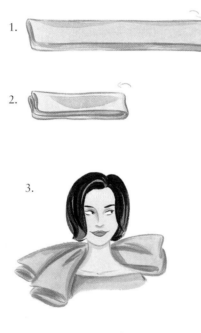

Neck wrap #3.

1. Lay a square scarf down so it looks like a diamond with two flat edges.

2. Fold the flat corners down to the center of the scarf.

3. Put the center of the scarf on your throat and wrap it twice around your neck. Flip the ends over one another and adjust as desired.

CAN'T TIE? JUST HANG!

Fold an oblong scarf lengthwise either once or twice and tuck it under the collar of your shirt, jacket or coat. The hanging ends, which shouldn't hang lower than the top of your hipbone, will instantly elongate your figure. This is a great look for wide and short-waisted figures. Another version: Fold a 36″ square diagonally and drape over your coat, with the point in the back.

SARONGS

The sarong—a truly amazing, versatile garment that can become everything from a beach wrap to a halter dress to a mini skirt—baffles many women. Here are three ways to wear a sarong:

The following two skirt styles—simple and wrap-and-tuck—can be worn either long or short. For a short length, simply fold the sarong horizontally to the desired length before you start the tying process. For a longer style, leave the sarong unfolded.

Simple.

1. Holding the fabric horizontally behind you, position the center of the sarong in the small of your back.

2. Adjust your grip so that you've got about three inches of the top of the sarong in both hands.

3. Pull the sarong around your sides, so that your fists meet just below your belly button and tie the two pieces of fabric into a double knot. Adjust to the side or back as desired.

Wrap-and-tuck.

1. Hold the fabric horizontally behind you with outstretched arms. Then fold one side tightly over your body to below your belly button and hold.

2. Extend the other end of the sarong straight out from your hip, making sure that the fabric is as taut as possible. Wrap over the other side, taking care to keep everything snug against your hips.

3. Secure the sarong by tucking about three inches of the top layer into the bottom layer.

This can be adapted to make a dress by moving the top of the sarong from the small of the back to just under the arms. Fold one half over your body and secure under the opposite arm. Then continue as described above.

Strapless dress.

1. Lay the sarong horizontally over your breasts.

2. Pull the fabric around you and swap the ends of the sarong in your hands behind your back. Then wrap the fabric back to front, with your left hand up slightly and right hand down slightly.

3. Tie the sarong in a high double knot off the left side.

BELTS

As the one accessory that sits squarely on a figure hot zone, the belt can cause some angst. Have no fear. When used with know-how, a belt in the right width and color can actually help slim and add balance to your figure. Beyond its figure-enhancing uses, however, a belt is another quick and easy way to add panache to your clothing. A belt with a knock-out buckle or a decorative strap can actually *make* an outfit, and even a simple neutral with a classic buckle can add a welcome finishing touch.

Belt flattery.

A belt fits if it can be buckled comfortably into the third hole.

Belting your waist to look smaller just makes your hips and bust look bigger.

If you don't wear belts—or wear them lower on your hips—consider having the loops on your pants removed for a cleaner look.

Color. Dark or matte-finish belts are more slimming than light-colored or shiny ones.

Belts that blend in with a garment are most slimming.

Wear a belt in a contrasting color only if your waistline is an asset.

Width. Wider belts are less versatile than thinner ones.

A classic 3/4-inch width flatters most women.

If you're heavy, busty, short, petite or have waist or hip problems, a thin belt toned to what you're wearing is the best choice.

Buckle. A leather-covered buckle is classic and versatile.

A small, simple, matte buckle is most slimming.

A decorative buckle will draw attention to your waistline.

A fancy or elaborate buckle functions as a grand piece of jewelry—so keep other pieces (as well as your outfit) spare.

Belts for body types.

THICK-WAISTED OR HEAVY
Under an open jacket or cardigan, wear a narrow belt toned to your outfit.

SHORT-WAISTED
Wear your belt and pants or skirt a little lower than your natural waistline. Match the belt to your top, in order to elongate your torso. (Make sure that your belt is the width of your waistband, so that no color shows over the top of the belt and interrupts the line.) Stick to narrow styles, or try a hip belt.

LONG-WAISTED
Match your belt to the color of the bottom to add length to your legs. Women with this figure can wear wider belts.

SHOPPING TIPS

Don't buy a belt without trying it on. You want to make sure that it is neither too long nor too short and that it fits in your belt loops. High-quality belts are made from soft, flexible leather (or other material), have clean edges, consistent stitching and a finished backside.

Glasses and Sunglasses.

> My look is attainable. Women can look like Audrey Hepburn by flipping out their hair and buying the large sunglasses and the little sleeveless dresses.
>
> AUDREY HEPBURN

Jennifer Lopez looks cool and casual in her oversize shades.

Sunglasses have symbolized Hollywood and high-fashion cool since the 1940s. Who can think of Audrey Hepburn or Jackie O. without their oversize sunglasses? But even regular prescription glasses have had a complete image makeover relatively recently. Marian-the-librarian hornrims made way for glasses as chic as any fashion accessory. Because glasses alter your look perhaps more than anything else you put on, it's important to use extra care in selecting them. By shopping in a specialty store staffed with trained opticians, you're more likely to end up with a flattering pair that also fits well and has the lenses best suited for your needs: Do you live in a sunny climate? Drive a lot? Sit in front of a computer all day? Whatever your lifestyle, the perfect pair is waiting for you. All you have to do is look.

Flattery.

Finding the right eyeglasses for your face is a three-step process. These guidelines are to help you get started and are not meant to be definitive.

General Tips:

Update your glasses about every two years.

Check yourself out in a full-length mirror—to make sure that your glasses match your body's proportions.

If you have strong cheekbones, your glasses shouldn't cover them.

Frames that turn downward can be aging, while those with some upsweep can help lift the face.

When in doubt, look at oval frames; they flatter almost everyone.

For the most part (but not in every case) the best shape for your eyeglasses is the opposite of the shape of your face.

Step 1: Facial Shape

Oval

Almost any eyeglass shape works with an oval face. Generally, however, the frames should be as wide or slightly wider than the broadest part of your face. Be sure that the size of the glasses works in proportion to the size of your head and features.

Oblong

Oval or other shapes that have a strong horizontal line help to shorten the face and soften its angles. Decorative detailing on the temples can add width. A low bridge (which shortens the nose) and low temples (which shorten the face) can be flattering.

Round

Wide ovals, cat-eye styles and angular shapes will diminish fullness. Also look for frames that are wider than they are tall and that have higher temples.

Heart-Shaped

Oval, slightly rounded or butterfly shapes help soften these faces.

Inverted Triangle

Look for frames with emphasis on the top—like aviators or those with a half rim. Glasses should angle inward toward the bottom.

Square

Curved shapes that are more horizontal than vertical will soften the angles of this facial shape. Avoid frames with a flat bottom.

Step 2: Facial Details and Coloring

Long Nose

A low, prominent bridge breaks up the length of the nose. Ornamentation at the temples widens the face and can help to divert attention from the nose. Dark colors are a good choice.

Small Nose

Choose glasses with a high bridge, in order to expose as much of the nose as possible. Delicate metal frames are usually more flattering than heavier plastic ones.

Wide Nose

A dark bridge can help elongate a wide nose, but the bridge should be thin and simple, so as not to call attention to itself. High temples help to draw the face upward. Rimless or metal frames with adjustable nose pads are the most flattering. Avoid plastic frames, which can make your nose look pinched.

Close-Set Eyes

A clear bridge and ornamentation at the temples help to widen the face. Avoid large frames.

Wide-Set Eyes

A dark bridge makes the eyes appear closer together. Larger rimless or plastic styles work best.

Eyebrows

The most flattering glasses follow the curve of the eyebrows. Also, be sure that your brows are visible *above* the frame.

Coloring

The colors that flatter you in clothing will flatter you in glasses. For the most part, look for something that contrasts with your skin tone. Those with pale skin often look great in dark glasses, but it is difficult to generalize. Matching your frames to your hair or highlights is a sure winner.

Step 3: Fit

Crooked glasses are a comedy staple, but ill-fitting glasses don't just look silly—they're bad for your eyes. Glasses that don't fit well can lead to squinting, tearing, and even headaches and nausea. To keep glasses in shape, avoid wearing them on top of your head or taking them off to the side with one hand—both of which will stretch them. Have your glasses refitted several times a year. Even if all you ever wear is nonprescription sunglasses, it's worth a trip to the optician.

OVERALL
Eyewear should fit comfortably on the face, without pinching or slipping.

BRIDGE
Glasses should be perfectly balanced on the nose, with the nose pads lying flat.

LENSES
The eye should be either in the middle of the lens or centered in the top third of the lens.

SIDEPIECES
To make sure that your glasses lie straight, the sidepieces should rest comfortably on top of your ears, not above them, and they should not dig into your head. One ear may be slightly higher than the other, so be sure the adjustment of your glasses takes that into account.

OVERHANG
The ends of the sidepieces should not stick out of the hair or be visible behind the ears.

GREAT MOMENTS IN
SUNGLASSES

Cover your eyes and suddenly you're an enigma—which is why sunglasses are so cool. They allow the wearer to observe without being observed, and they close the windows to the soul, allowing almost no emotion to show through. All this—and, in some cases, their ability to conceal the sins of last night—have made shades the number one accessory for any self-respecting screen idol—or paparazzi target. Take a look:

1. Jacqueline Kennedy Onassis, ca. late 1970s.
2. Madonna in *Desperately Seeking Susan*, 1985.
3. Audrey Hepburn in *Breakfast at Tiffany's*, 1961.
4. Angelina Jolie in *Tomb Raider*, 2001.
5. Sue Lyon in *Lolita*, 1962.

LENSES

Types and coatings.

Depending on your needs, here are a few types of lenses and coatings that may help you to see better:

Polarized. Highly recommended for people who do a lot of driving, these lenses reduce glare by absorbing reflections from horizontal surfaces, such as highways or a pool of water.

Photochromic. These lenses are light-sensitive: They get darker as they are exposed to ultraviolet light, thus allowing the wearer to use them both indoors and out.

Polycarbonate. Made from a light-weight plastic, polycarbonate lenses offer superior impact-resistance, making them great for people who wear their glasses or sunglasses while playing sports.

Anti-Reflective (AR) coating. A lens treatment designed to block reflected light, AR coating is often applied to prescription glasses to stop light from reflecting off the surfaces of the lens. It makes the lens itself less reflective and allows for better visibility when working under fluorescent lighting, at a computer or while driving at night.

Scratch-Resistant coating. Just as the name says, this coating helps cut down on the scratches that occur during normal wear.

UV protection. This lens treatment protects the eyes from harmful UV rays and can be added to both regular glasses and sunglasses.

Mirror-Coated lenses. These lenses have a thin metallic coating that helps protect their wearer from infrared radiation and reflects light away from the eyes—making them more comfortable to wear in bright light or high heat than noncoated lenses.

Gradient tinted lenses. Since these sunglasses are dark at the top and gradually lighten as they get to the bottom, they can be useful for cutting down on overhead glare.

Double gradient tinted lenses. These are darker at the top and bottom, but lighter in the center, cutting down on glare from both above and below.

Color.

Rose-colored glasses are said to make the world seem like a more beautiful place—here's what certain other colored lenses can do. Any of these lenses can be polarized, to help reduce glare.

Green-gray. This is the most popular color for lenses, because it filters light evenly and distorts color the least. These lenses are best for bright, sunny days.

Brown to yellow. These lenses distort color somewhat, but allow for higher contrast by filtering out blue light. They are helpful for driving on overcast or hazy days and at dusk.

Purple, pink or blue. Lenses in these colors should be saved primarily for making a fashion statement, because they interfere with color perception.

SUN PROTECTION

Sunglasses aren't just about attitude—they have a serious job to do. Overexposure to the sun can cause damage to the cornea and the retina, as well as to the delicate skin around the eye. Sunglasses can prevent such damage—provided they offer UV protection. You should buy glasses that block 95 to 99 percent of UVB rays (which penetrate deep into the eyes) and 60 percent of UVA rays (which are responsible for surface damage to the eyes and skin). If you're buying from a specialty sunglasses store, the optician will be able to tell you how much protection each lens offers. If you are buying in a clothing, department or drugstore, consult the label. The FDA regulates nonprescription sunglasses and requires that manufacturers provide such labeling for consumer protection. This is the most compelling reason not to buy sunglasses from a street vendor: Often those glasses are not labeled, and may offer very little protection even if they are very dark or very large. In fact, some experts think that dark lenses without UV protection are especially dangerous, because a dilated pupil allows more harmful rays to penetrate.

Swimsuits.

As Jinx in *Die Another Day*, Halle Berry made a splash in this suit—a replica of the one worn by Ursula Andress in *Dr. No*.

People shop for a bathing suit with more care than they do a husband or wife. The rules are the same. Look for something you'll feel comfortable wearing. Allow for room to grow.

ERMA BOMBECK

As dreaded events go, shopping for a swimsuit usually ranks up there with a trip to the dentist. The endless try-ons under fluorescent lighting—and the mere thought of having to walk down the beach in next to nothing—can leave even the most confident woman on the brink of despair. But if you find the right suit, it can flatter your figure. Start by experimenting with styles you've dismissed in the past. Although full coverage may feel more secure, often a smaller suit can be quite becoming. Then, as with your clothing, make strategic use of color, pattern, detailing and shine to draw attention where you want it and divert it from the places you don't. It may take a little time and experimentation to find exactly the right suit for you, but the confidence you'll feel once you do will make it worth the effort.

Flattery.

Bathing Suit Basics

Here's a recap of the shopping tools for everyday clothes that you can use in your search for a flattering swimsuit:

Color. Use darker colors on areas you'd like to slim and bright or light colors in places you want to showcase. Certainly an all-black suit is a slimming and safe bet, but you may be able to do even better. Say it's your hips you're looking to play down. A suit with black on the bottom and a lighter color on the top (a colorblock or some piping) will help draw attention up and away from your hips. Another good trick: Look for an otherwise bright suit with dark insets on the sides. They will make your figure look both slimmer and more sculpted.

Prints. Pay attention to a print's size, colors and placement. Prints with darker backgrounds are usually more slimming. Allover patterns with lots of swirling movement keep the eye from focusing on any one area.

Shine. Matte fabrics are the most slimming; shiny, reflective ones make things appear larger. If you like the shine but not its effects, look for something shiny in a muted or dark color—or try a matte suit with shiny detail.

Details. Bows, belts, shirring, embroidery, beading and ties—all of these details are attention-grabbers, so use them on places where you'd like the eye to linger.

Less is more. Running for cover is not the best way to deal with figure flaws—especially with swimwear. Just as hiding under a voluminous shirt makes a large bust look even larger, draping a piece of fabric over an ample derrière may draw unwanted attention to that very spot. The skirted suit is one example: Women with large hips often assume that this style is their only option. Yet the skirt on this swimsuit often ends at the widest part of the hips or thighs, making the area appear even larger. A much better choice is a suit with a higher-cut leg opening (which elongates the legs) and with detailing or a bright color on top (to attract the eye). As long as a suit fits properly and showcases your assets, bare is usually more beautiful.

Curvy

DETAILS:
If your curves are ample, try wrapped styles or those with allover patterns.

Accentuate the waistline with belts, mesh insets, chevron patterns and diagonals.

Use side-shirring and dark side insets to showcase your shape.

Support the bust with an underwire or built-in cups; a shelf bra may not be enough.

Try halter necklines, to help with shaping.

Choose suits with sufficient coverage at the bust and derrière.

Go with high-cut leg holes, to elongate legs.

AVOID:
Suits without enough support or those that don't fit properly in the bust and derrière.

Broad Shoulders

DETAILS:
Use V-necks or scoop necklines to lengthen the torso.

Look for vertical details, diagonals or chevron patterns, all of which make the body seem longer.

Look for straps that hit mid-shoulder, to cut off breadth.

Try wider straps which, can make the shoulders appear less broad.

AVOID:
Racerback suits and halter necklines.

Full Bust

DETAILS:
Look for built-in support from cups or an underwire.

Get support from wider straps, densely woven fabrics and a high Lycra content.

Try a halter suit with built-in support—good for shaping.

Use details like ruffles, shirring and draping below the chest, to draw the eye downward.

Choose suits with dark, solid colors on top and lighter colors below.

Consider dark, slimming panels at the sides of the bust.

Use lower necklines and vertical details to help elongate the silhouette.

AVOID:
Suits that lack support or coverage or suits with belts (unless your waist is small and your torso long).

Small Bust

DETAILS:
Choose string bikinis or other soft styles (if you are not looking to enhance your bust).

If you'd like to add something extra to your bustline, try a bra-top style, an underwire, a push-up top or light padding.

Use bright colors and details—like shirring—at the top of a suit, to give the illusion of a larger bust.

Look for lower necklines.

AVOID:
Overly structured suits and obvious padding in the bust.

Tummy

DETAILS:
Look for diagonal lines and chevron patterns.

Add verticals in the form of V-necklines, piping, patterns or seaming.

Look for a lighter color or a bit of detailing at the top. Lower necklines can also be flattering.

You might consider an ombré design that starts out light at the top and gradually gets darker toward the bottom.

Choose side-shirring or dark side panels that curve in at the waist.

If wearing a two-piece, look for bottoms with higher waistbands.

Look for a high Lycra content, to help with control.

Consider suits by manufacturers such as Miraclesuit that have built-in control panels.

AVOID:
Anything that cuts across the body horizontally and two-piece suits with bottoms that dig into your tummy.

Short-Waisted

DETAILS:
In a two-piece, look for bottoms that ride lower than your natural waistline.

To elongate the torso, create strong verticals with details, seaming and color.

A high neckline makes the torso appear longer.

Darker side panels—or ones with a strong color that runs vertically down the center of the panel—will help create a longer silhouette.

AVOID:
High-waisted bikini bottoms and suits with horizontal detailing in the midsection.

Long-Waisted

DETAILS:
Look for two-piece suits or one-piece styles made especially for long torsos: they will be the most comfortable.

Consider a "tankini" if you want coverage without pulling. The horizontal break in coverage also helps the body look more proportional.

Look for a horizontal line across the midsection—such as a belt, stripes, patterns, or insets in a lighter color—to help balance the figure.

To increase the appearance of leg length, try higher leg cuts.

AVOID:
One-piece suits that are too short in the body and boy-leg briefs.

Bottom-Heavy

DETAILS:
Wear an attention-grabbing color or detail at the bustline.

Keep the bottom of the suit dark and matte.

Consider an ombré pattern that graduates from light on the top to dark on the bottom.

Use V-necks, along with vertical stripes, prints and details, to elongate the torso.

Try strapless styles, which create a strong horizontal line and balance the figure.

Consider Empire-waist suits.

Use darker side panels on the bottom, to take a few inches off of your hips.

Try side shirring, to sculpt the body.

AVOID:
Bottoms that dig into your flesh and skirted suits that end at your largest part.

Fit.

Swimsuit sizing can seem like one of life's cruel jokes. Generally, to get a good fit, you need to buy a suit that is a size or two larger than your dress size. Once in the dressing room, be sure to move around. Lift your arms, bend and sit down—making sure that everything stays covered.

Straps

Swimsuit straps should lie comfortably on your shoulders. If they dig at all, try on the next size up. Conversely, if they fall down, you may need a smaller size or a different style. Move around to make sure that tie straps stay tied.

Body

The torso portion of a one-piece should lie perfectly flat without puckering near the seams or pulling at the crotch, bust or straps.

Bust

Lift your arms to be sure that you've got enough coverage and that the bra doesn't creep up on you. Make certain that you can adjust the straps to feel comfortable and secure. If you're looking at a suit with an underwire or built-in cups, you need to be especially careful: The underwire in your bathing suit should fit as well as the one in your bra—completely surrounding the bottom half of the breast and not sitting on any breast tissue. As for cups, your breasts should fill them completely without spilling over. Since it can be difficult to find a suit in your body size that really fits your bust, look for manufacturers that offer bra sizing. If you can't find one, choose a style with a built-in shelf bra (which is easier to fit) and adjustable straps at the back and neck (which will allow you to fasten the suit tighter for more support).

Leg Openings

Make sure that leg openings—and the waistbands of two-piece suits—are not puckering or digging into your skin. If the suit is digging, go up a size. If you're looking for more coverage, a different style is the answer, not a different size. The most flattering leg opening for most people falls an inch below the top of the hipbone, so start there and experiment. Also check out your rear view—to make sure that you have as much coverage as you want.

CARE

Chlorine, sand, salt, sweat, sun and lotions all eat away at the fabric or fade the color of swimsuits, which is why they need to be replaced so often—depending on how much you use your suit and how well you take care of it.

To make a bathing suit last as long as possible, rinse it out with mild soap and cold water after each wear, and let it drip-dry out of the sun. Do not use harsh detergents (which make the suit stiff), hot water (which fades the color), or a dryer (which breaks down the Lycra and ruins the fit).

GREAT MOMENTS IN
BATHING SUITS

For all of the angst they cause, swimsuits can also evoke some of life's most pleasant moments: strolling down the beach, splashing in the surf, diving into a cool pool on a hot day. This is the stuff that vacations and weekends are made of—simple, relaxing and utterly carefree. A few of our favorite Hollywood beach babes:

1. Annette Funicello posing for her "Muscle Beach Party" album cover, 1964.
2. Ursula Andress in *Dr. No*, 1962.
3. Bo Derek in *10*, 1979.
4. Elizabeth Taylor in *Suddenly Last Summer*, 1959.
5. Phoebe Cates in *Fast Times at Ridgemont High*, 1982.

Special
Occasion
Style.

Special Occasions.

Nicole Kidman is ready for the red carpet in Gaultier Paris at the 2003 Oscars.

> "What shall I wear?" is society's second most frequently asked question. The first is "Do you really love me?" No matter what one replies to either, it is never accepted as settling the issue.
>
> JUDITH MARTIN

The last-minute dash for something to wear to a special event is practically a shopper's rite of passage. But as with all difficult experiences, we can learn something from this one, too: Be prepared. Although it may sound impossible to have something perfectly appropriate, sufficiently festive and totally gorgeous on hand for every event that arises, it's not. As a matter of fact, one simple and timeless dark dress can work for many different occasions—weddings, funerals, graduation ceremonies and religious services—with nothing more than a switch of accessories. Once you have this versatile workhorse in hand, you can add more colorful and interesting pieces as time goes by. You can even relax and shop for a new outfit the weekend before the big event, because your fallback dress eliminates all the pressure. It will still be last-minute shopping—but you'll be working with a net.

SPECIAL EVENT DRESSING

All-out affairs call for your all-out dress, but what about those more common occasions? A date, a party, a funeral, a religious service? When a dressy, but not too dressy, outfit is what's called for? The best way to figure out what to wear is to think about your "goal" look. Do you want to look sexy? Nonchalant? Subdued? Feminine? By identifying what feels right for the occasion, you'll be able to weed out things that are too skimpy or shiny or too tailored or staid and zero in on the types of suits, dresses and separates that are most appropriate. Still, buying an outfit for just one occasion isn't always the smartest use of your money. So, here are five outfits that can do double, triple and even quadruple duty.

Daytime wedding

Graduation

Religious service

Office party

Funeral

The goal: quiet and chic. A dark sheath dress is something you should always have in your closet. This dress can practically do it all. It's staid enough for solemn events and religious services, but simple enough to be "glitzed up" for an office party, daytime wedding or graduation celebration.

Formal cocktails

Evening wedding

New Year's Eve

The goal: simple—yet sizzling.
Special occasions with friends (as opposed to colleagues) call for some *oomph*—but that doesn't mean you have to find an entrance-maker every time you're invited to an opening, reception or party. A simple dress with a bit of shine or with a single interesting detail can be smashing—and it won't leave you feeling so conspicuous that you'd hesitate to wear it again. For an alluring look, show a little skin. If a backless dress or one with a plunging V-neck is too much for you, go strapless. It's sexy and classy, and almost everyone's shoulders are worthy of the attention. You can always carry a wrap if you're worried about your upper arms. A shawl will cover fleshy parts, while still letting the bare neck and shoulders do their thing.

Daytime wedding

Graduation

Religious service

The goal: festive—but not too dramatic. A suit, which is inherently conservative, is a nice option. Look for a shapely style with a nipped waist and other ladylike detailing such as bracelet sleeves or a shiny fabric, and choose a color that will make an impact—like a deep jewel tone, an icy pastel or a sophisticated off-white.

Wedding

Baby shower

Birthday party

The goal: informal—but feminine.
Opt for pieces that are easygoing without being too casual—like a skirt or dress with movement or drape. Fabrics should be rich and luxurious, in light-hearted colors.

Party

Date

Reunion

The goal: effortless, with lots of impact. If you want to turn heads without looking like you're trying too hard, pants are a good bet. Choose a pair in a sexy cut and add a blouse made from a feminine fabric—like chiffon or satin—that shows just a teaser of skin. For the perfect finishing touch, reach for the high heels. They'll add a subtle but sexy sashay to your walk.

DAY-TO-NIGHT GUIDELINES

Wondering what to wear if an event is scheduled right after work? Instead of lugging an entire outfit with you, just bring along a few well-chosen accessories or underpinnings and you'll be able to turn your everyday workwear into snazzy evening attire.

Keep it simple. The outfit you're dressing up should be flourish-free, but cut from a fine fabric. A few "easy-to-morph" looks include a well-cut suit, a sheath, a white shirt and trousers, or a silk blouse and pencil skirt. Fabrics to look for include gabardine, crêpe or anything with a slight sheen.

Add contrasts. Contrast adds instant sex appeal to an outfit. If you're wearing a suit (which is masculine), pair it with a feminine bustier top. Also consider contrasting day elements, like a dress made from wool, with those that are fancier, like strappy shoes or dangling earrings.

Show some skin. If you're wearing a button-down shirt, open a few buttons or change into something bare—like a satin camisole. If your daywear comes up to your neck, then put the focus on your legs with a pair of sexy shoes.

Accessorize. Swap tailored pumps or boots for something more delicate and higher-heeled. Add one great piece of jewelry—like chandelier earrings, a silver cuff or a chunky necklace—and trade in your tote or briefcase for a small evening bag with a bit of sparkle.

Vivica A. Fox's pearls, heels and judicious unbuttoning get a basic day look ready for a party.

Detailing such as embroidery and fringing give Julia Roberts's outfit 24-hour appeal.

Charlize Theron's rich red sweater and leather skirt amp up simple day cuts; bare sandals finish the job.

Travel.

Sophia Loren waiting for her flight in classic style.

On a long journey, even a straw weighs heavy.

SPANISH PROVERB

Nothing makes a woman weigh her priorities like packing for a trip. The struggle between wanting to be prepared for every eventuality or fashion whim and needing to actually carry your luggage makes packing a serious game of give and take. While you know that bringing less will make travel easier, it's tough not to wonder whether, come Saturday night, you'll be yearning for those orange pumps or that *other* black top. But packing doesn't necessarily mean doing without. With a little planning and organization, you can create a wardrobe of mix-and-match basics that cover all of your needs—while still leaving room for some great accessories and even one or two special pieces.

Planning.

Do your research. Before you start deciding what to bring, find out what's ahead of you. Read guidebooks and check out travel Web sites for local customs and other information that will help you decide what to take. Next, check the weather, to be sure that you're prepared for any eventuality. Last, call your hotel, to see whether they provide toiletries, a hairdryer, an iron or any other amenities that you can then leave behind. If you might make use of them, ask if they have laundry facilities.

Make a list. Make a list, day by day, of all of your planned activities—shopping, horseback riding, sunbathing, dinner, dancing, a play, etc.—and then pick out what you'd like to wear to each event. Later, after you've edited your clothing (see below), make revisions that reflect your final choices. This will give you a record of what you packed, should anything happen to your luggage, and will serve as a starting point when packing for your next trip.

Edit your choices. Once you've decided what you'd *like* to bring, lay everything out and create ensembles. This is the easiest way to make sure that you've got all of the pieces and accessories you'll need—with nothing unnecessary included. Once that's done, go back over everything again and see if any pieces are redundant—say, two black cardigans. Limiting yourself to one base color will force you to mix and match and to think of ways to get more than one wearing out of almost everything you bring.

Think about your shoes. Shoes can be heavy and unwieldy, so choose wisely. You'll always need a pair of comfortable walking shoes and probably something a little dressier for evening. Try to choose pairs that go with the majority of your clothing. Don't bring any outfit that calls for its own pair of shoes—unless, of course, you are traveling for a special event, such as a wedding.

Add color. While your base color should be a solid neutral, you can brighten and alter your look with scarves, thin knits and T-shirts. They are crushable and take up little room in your suitcase. Jewelry, too, will make your outfits more interesting—but don't pack anything that you can't risk losing.

Try on everything. Put on each outfit, to make sure that everything looks as good as it does in your mind's eye. Check for stains, fallen hems or missing buttons.

Have toiletries at the ready. Keep a travel kit packed with miniature bottles of shampoo, conditioner, moisturizer, toothpaste, a toothbrush and other essentials. When you return from your trip, refill everything before putting the kit away for your next trip.

Packing.

Close your closures. Button all buttons and zip all zippers, to ensure that all plackets, cuffs, flies and collars lie flat.

Take precautions against wrinkling. Turn dresses, jackets and shirts inside-out (inverted creases are less visible) and stuff jacket and blouse sleeves with tissue paper. Then line everything in plastic before folding. Plastic garbage bags or the plastic wrap that protects your drycleaning are the best wrinkle-fighters going. You can put plastic on top and underneath and fold as usual; put plastic inside of a piece of clothing, fold lengthwise and roll; or put a cleaner's bag on a hanger, put your piece over it, cover with another bag, fold into thirds and place on top of other clothes in your luggage.

Do the roll-and-stuff. Small items (underwear, sleepwear, belts, socks, scarves) and anything that is wrinkle-resistant (jeans, T-shirts, knits) should be rolled up and stuffed into dead spaces within the suitcases—the corners, between stacks of clothing, and inside shoes.

Layer. Pack your heaviest items first. The things you will need when you arrive go in last, so they're the first to be unpacked.

Fill 'er up. Leaving lots of empty space in a suitcase will wrinkle your clothes just as badly as overstuffing it, so use the right size case for your needs. If you are planning to shop on your trip, pack a collapsible duffle, instead of leaving loads of room in your bag.

Preparing for air travel.

Dress in nonconstrictive clothing. The idea is to be comfortable but presentable and to wear pieces that can be mixed and matched with the rest of your clothes. Fabrics should be wrinkle-resistant—like those blended with Lycra, tropical-weight wools, cottons and knits. Pants are usually a better option than skirts.

Wear your bulkiest items. If you need a winter coat, a suit, boots or a rain jacket, wearing them on the plane will save you from having to stuff them into a suitcase.

Wear comfortable shoes. Feet swell when you fly, so avoid pointed shoes or tight boots, which could constrict blood flow and make your first vacation steps painful ones.

Carry a shawl. A shawl takes up very little room in a carry-on bag and is useful as a blanket.

Stock up on rehydration items. The air in airplane cabins is notoriously dry. Keep yourself looking and feeling good by stashing moisturizer, lip balm, eye drops and bottled water in your purse or carry-on.

Going from cold to hot? Dress in several thin layers under your coat. Once you arrive, you can strip down, stuffing the extras into your carry-on bag and draping the coat over your arm.

DESTINATION CHECKLISTS

What you should pack is based on your style, your destination and the activities you have planned. Use the following checklists as starting points. They can tell you the kinds of things you'll want to pack, as well as how much you're likely to need. (All three wardrobes are based on a five-day trip.)

Beach.

One cotton sundress

One gauzy or cotton skirt

One pair of loose-fitting pants

One pair of shorts

One beach cover-up

Four to six T-shirts

Two bare cotton tops, such as camisoles or tank tops

A light sweater or jacket

Bathing suit

Sun hat

Sunglasses

Flip-flops for the beach

Jeweled sandals with a small heel for evening

Walking shoes for shopping and touring

Sunblock

Dangling earrings and bangle bracelets in metal, turquoise or coral

A beach bag

A small bag for evening (this could be a spiffy cosmetics case)

City.

Tailored pants

A skirt with special detail

Five to seven T-shirts

Two dressy tops

A lightweight sweater that can be worn casually or with the skirt

A layering sweater and jacket, if the weather calls for them

Rubber-sole, low-heel shoes for shopping and touring

Shoes with a small heel for evenings out

Umbrella

Raincoat

Sunglasses

Hoop earrings for day and night   or something smaller for day and more dangly for night

A shoulder bag for daytime

A small bag for evening

Country.

Jeans

A skirt in corduroy or cotton

Shorts (for warm-weather destinations)

Four long-sleeved T-shirts

Four short-sleeved T-shirts

A heavy denim shirt that can double as a jacket

One layering sweater

One heavy sweater for cold nights, if needed

A windbreaker or jacket

Warm socks for night, if needed

A bathing suit and cover-up, if needed

Sneakers or hiking boots

Boots or flats to wear with the skirt for evenings

Hoop earrings or those with a Southwestern flair

A leather or suede bag that can work for both day and night

CARRY-ON WISDOM

Losing a piece of luggage is an annoyance, but losing a piece of luggage that contained your heirloom necklace, your prescriptions, or an irreplaceable outfit is a tragedy. Generally, you should pack your health and beauty essentials, as well as any valuables, in your carry-on case. Here are some items to keep with you:

Medicines (prescriptions and over-the-counter drugs)

Extra eyeglasses (and your prescription)

Business papers

Travel documents

Receipts for everything you bought on your trip

Anything breakable, such as a camera or a fragile souvenir

Jewelry

Address book

A set of underwear and nightclothes

The toiletries you use daily

A swimsuit, if you're going someplace warm

A suit, if you're on a business trip

The special dress or outfit, if you're going to a special event

Maternity.

Sarah Jessica Parker proved that bare skin and a flirty dress are very becoming on a pregnant woman.

Childbirth is more admirable than conquest, more amazing than self-defense, and as courageous as either one.

GLORIA STEINEM

Ironically, one of the happiest times in a woman's life can also be the most sartorially frustrating. Within weeks of getting the good news, your clothes start to feel tight, and before you know it, bras don't fit, pants won't button, and your undies are pulling like crazy. It's tough to feel beautiful when you're swollen up and tired out—and no amount of cooing from your nearest and dearest is going to change that. Looking your best, however, is a small step in the right direction. Luckily, today there are many stylish offerings. As a matter of fact, it's possible to find the same styles you wore prepregnancy (including the latest jeans) in maternity versions—which could go a long way to making you feel like the hot mama everyone keeps telling you that you are.

TIPS FOR A STYLISH PREGNANCY

By wearing a deep V-neck, Claudia Schiffer put her newly acquired cleavage to good use.

WEAR YOUR REGULAR CLOTHES AS LONG AS POSSIBLE.

Whether out of excitement over a new pregnancy or due to panic over diminishing choices in their wardrobes, many women buy their maternity clothes too early. The body does swell a bit during the first trimester, but most women don't get large until the second. Any new clothes that fit during the early weeks may not carry you through your entire pregnancy. Also, wearing maternity clothes during the early stages can make you look much larger, since they are cut with different proportions in mind. If you have clothing of varying sizes in your closet, now is the time to make use of the largest size. Many women find ingenious ways of hooking their pants closed with safety pins and a rubber band and then hiding everything under a loose-fitting top. If you're not comfortable walking out of the house like that, buy a few pieces that are a size or two larger than you normally wear. Just don't invest any serious cash—you'll want to save that for the real maternity pieces you'll buy later.

DON'T CHANGE YOUR STYLE.

When your belly does start growing, think about the three to five items in your pre-pregnancy wardrobe that you can't live without. Then look for them in maternity styles. Invest exclusively in pieces like a suit, dressy pants and a dress. Fill in with knits and T-shirts that can be bought on the cheap without looking it.

DRESS IN ONE COLOR FROM HEAD TO TOE.

The most slimming and pulled-together look is monochromatic. Match tops to bottoms and bottoms to hose and shoes. Buying in one hue also streamlines your shopping trips and saves you money, since everything goes together.

Catherine Zeta-Jones' monochromatic outfit looked both slim and pulled together.

SHOW SOME SKIN.

Sleeveless tops and low-cut shirts that flaunt your newly acquired cleavage can be alluring. If you're not thrilled with your arms, wear bracelet or three-quarter-length sleeves to flash a hint of bare skin. Skirts that hit above the knee, even if that's not your usual length, seem to offset the belly well and flatter most pregnant women. Try one on and see if you should be trading up. Of course, think twice about baring flesh at the office. While showing your knees isn't going to make your colleagues blush, wearing a T-shirt that allows a glimpse of your naked belly may. Save it for off-hours.

SHOW OFF YOUR BELLY.

Today's snug-fitting maternity styles flatter a pregnant body much more than the tent-like muumuus of yesteryear.

Heather Locklear's form-fitting dress celebrated her pregnancy instead of hiding it.

MAKE USE OF JEWELRY AND SCARVES.

They add color to your basics, direct attention to your glowing face, and make a few outfits seem like many more.

LOOK FOR COMFORTABLE FABRICS.

Your skin is sensitive, you're prone to overheating, and you're carrying around extra pounds—so avoid clothing that might add to your discomfort. Lightweight, natural fabrics, such as cotton and silk, will feel nice next to your skin; and since they breathe, they are much cooler than synthetics. Now is also the time to consider Lycra blends, which work particularly well on a changing figure.

BUY NEW UNDERWEAR.

Your underthings will demand attention like never before. You'll need at least one new bra in the first trimester, and in the second (if not earlier) your stock of panties will become totally useless. (See box at right for details on what to look for.)

BUY SOME COMFORTABLE SHOES.

Many women rejoice over their growing cleavage—but growing feet are another matter. No matter how you try to ignore it, however, the size or two being added to your tootsies will demand your attention. Treat yourself to a pair of low-heeled shoes that have some width in the toe. In summer, sandals look chic. In winter, look for boots with elastic sides (they'll hide swollen ankles), loafers or chic but supportive flats.

PUT A LITTLE EXTRA EFFORT INTO YOUR HAIR AND MAKEUP.

This is not meant to make life harder, but to help you feel good about yourself. If you're feeling blue because of surging hormones or self-conscious because of your rapidly changing body, put the focus on the glowing skin and lustrous hair that are often a part of pregnancy, too.

THE SMALL STUFF

Swimwear. Most maternity lines offer chic swimwear, but the choices may be limited. If you can't find what you want, buying from a regular manufacturer is an option. Be aware, however, that since these suits aren't cut for a pregnant woman's proportions, finding the right fit can be tough. Also, make sure that whatever you try on has enough support at the bust, in the form of a shelf bra or molded cups.

Bras. It's not unusual for the breasts to grow two sizes, in both cup and band, during pregnancy—making supportive bras a necessity. Not only do they provide greater comfort, but they also keep breast tissue from stretching (which can lead to sagging later on). Look for something that allows room for growth: Straps should be adjustable, and the closure should have at least three positions (when buying, fit yourself to the tightest). For many women, an underwire becomes uncomfortable, and an ill-fitting underwire can put undue stress on sensitive breast tissue. Wider straps and a wider band can provide the additional support you need. Be sure to pick a breathable fabric, like cotton, so as not to irritate sensitive skin.

Panties. Maternity undies come in all shapes and sizes, including bikinis and thongs. Whatever you buy, just be sure that it doesn't bind or dig and that the elastic doesn't irritate your skin.

Care, Repair and Storage.

Caring for luxury fabrics.

CASHMERE

Advice from Marc Aitelli, manager, and Lynn Riker, assistant manager, Ballantyne Cashmere, 965 Madison Avenue, New York, NY 10021 212.988.5252.

Care. Be wary of perfume or heavy antiperspirants, which can ruin delicate yarn. Some colognes and perfumes contain bleaching agents or alcohol. The white powder from antiperspirants can stain.

De-pill your sweaters with a D-Fuzz-It sweater/fabric comb (about $3.50), which is available at most sweater stores. Electric de-pilling machines may damage the fibers.

Remove stains with Ever Blum Cosmetic Stain Remover (about $10), available at most hardware or notions stores.

Cleaning vs. washing. Dry cleaning is OK, but handwashing is preferable. You can put cashmere in a washing machine that has a gentle cycle, using the same soaps and drying method described below. However, if your garment contains more than one color yarn, always dryclean it in case all the colors are not colorfast.

Here's how to handwash:
In cold water, dissolve one teaspoon of a lingerie wash, Ivory Liquid dishwashing soap, Prell or Johnson's baby shampoo. (Do not use any products that contain bleach, like Woolite.) If there are no stains, swish the sweater around for a few minutes. If there is an obvious stain, gently rub the sweater for a moment or two.

Roll the sweater in a clean white bath towel to absorb excess water. Do not wring dry.

Lay the sweater flat on a towel to dry, taking care to shape it.

If necessary, carefully steam out any wrinkles.

Storage. Clean cashmere garments before you store them. Moths and other insects are attracted to dirt and odors.

To store cashmere sweaters, fold them into plastic or canvas bags or boxes. Never hang them—the weight will stretch the delicate knit.

Pack sweaters with cedar blocks or in a cedar chest.

Repair. Rips can be mended professionally. Take your cashmere garment to a seamstress you trust or to a reweaver, such as The French-American Reweaving Company, 119 West 57th Street, Room 1406, New York, NY 10019 212.765.4670. (For more information on reweaving, see page 99.)

FUR

Advice from Keith Kaplan, executive director, Fur Information Council of America, 8424-A Santa Monica Boulevard #860, West Hollywood, CA 90069 323.848.7940; www.fur.org.

Care. Have fur items cleaned professionally once a year, and store them in a climate-controlled facility.

The oils in perfumes can damage fur, so make sure that any scent you wear is dry before you put on a fur.

If matting occurs, which may be more likely to happen with sheared furs, the garment should be taken to a furrier for proper treatment.

If your fur gets wet, shake it out and hang it in a dry space away from heat and sunlight. Any odor should dissipate. If it doesn't, take the piece to a furrier.

If you spill liquids on your fur, dab—do not rub—the excess moisture away, and have the garment professionally cleaned as soon as you can.

Cleaning. Don't try to clean fur at home or send it to your dry cleaners (unless they offer a fur cleaning service).

Professional furriers do their own cleaning or have an arrangement with a facility that specializes in fur cleaning and glazing. Unlike cloth, which is cleaned by immersion, fur is cleaned by abrasion. It is tumbled in a drum with sawdust that has been soaked in a specially formulated solution to absorb the dirt and oils. The garment is then glazed to bring out the sheen and make it soft and fluffy. Flat, curly furs, such as broadtail, are pressed with a special type of waxed paper to give them added sheen.

Some furs require special attention. These include white and light-colored furs like white mink, fox, chinchilla and ermine. Over time, sunlight can yellow these furs. To remedy this, a furrier will add a special bleach whitener to white furs or a brightener to pale furs.

Fur-trimmed garments should only be cleaned by a furrier.

Storage. Store furs in professional, climate-controlled storage facilities, to prevent the skins from drying out, as well as to protect against insects and heat damage. Make sure that your storage facility is temperature- and humidity-controlled. Ask about the settings. (Optimal is between 40 and 50 degrees, with humidity at 45 to 55 percent). Also, don't forget to ask about insurance coverage.

If you need to store your fur at home, place smaller pieces (hats or bags) in the refrigerator. Cover coats and jackets with some type of protective cloth (furriers can make you a silk or cotton bag) and hang on a padded hanger. While cedar chips can help protect fur from insect damage, they do nothing to keep garments from drying out.

Repair. If your fur needs mending, take it to a professional furrier. A proper repair involves removing the lining and sewing the hide with a heavy-duty needle and thread, from the inside.

If sections of fur get worn away, matching fur can be sewn in to replace it.

Fur can be remodeled if you don't like the style.

LEATHER

Advice from Chuck Strausser, owner, Perry Process, leather, suede and knitwear cleaning and care specialists, 427 East 74th Street, New York, NY 10021 212.628.8300.

Quality. Touch is the best way to measure quality. If the leather feels and looks good to you, buy it. Don't judge quality solely on price; very often, you may be paying for a designer name alone.

Make sure sewn-together pieces look uniform in color. If they don't, chances are they come from different dye lots and won't wear or fade uniformly.

If the garment smells, it's an indication that the leather wasn't prepared or tanned correctly.

Bleeding dye—often a problem with distressed leather—is a bad sign.

Stains. If your leather garment gets stained, it is best to take leather to a professional immediately. If that is impossible, do not rub, lightly blot the stain with water (unless your garment is made of pigskin, which is too fragile to risk any home remedy). Do not saturate leather, or you risk leaving a water mark.

Salt. Salt is the enemy. Wipe any salt stains with a damp cloth immediately and then take the garment to a professional cleaner as soon as you can. If untreated, salt stains can become permanent.

Wetness. If a leather garment gets wet, it's best to hang it on a wood hanger and allow it to dry naturally. Do not speed up the process with heat from a hair dryer or radiator, which will only dry out the leather and make it stiff.

Cleaning. Cleaning should be done by a professional, who will clean the garment evenly, use moisturizers to condition the leather, and make it look alive again.

Always point out stains and any damage when you take your leather in for cleaning.

There is always a slight change to leather—either in its color or texture—when it's cleaned. The tanning process stretches leather. When garments are cleaned, the tension is released and there is slight shrinkage.

If a cleaner promises that your garment will be returned exactly as it was, question his or her knowledge about cleaning leather garments.

If you have a two-piece outfit, take both pieces to be cleaned at the same time, so that they will wear evenly.

No matter what the care label says, take it to a leather professional for his or her opinion.

The cost of cleaning and removing stains can vary according to garment type and the labor involved. Perry Process, which is a high-end cleaner, charges $75 to clean skirts or pants and between $75 and $175 to clean jackets or shirts.

Suede. Freshen up suede at home with a brush made for suede. Gently rub the brush against the grain of the suede, in a circular motion. Never use any products that contain moisture to clean suede.

Distressed leather. The dye in any leather can be tricky, but distressed leathers will always look different after cleaning, which will probably change the appearance and location of distress marks, or even eliminate them. Discuss any risks with the cleaners before you turn the garment over to them.

Storage. Clean your leather garments at the end of the season, so that current stains and invisible spills don't oxidize over the period of storage, making them impossible to remove.

Store leather away from heat.

Don't cover leather garments with plastic. Leather needs to breathe and will dry out under plastic. Use a cloth garment bag or an old sheet instead—or don't cover it at all.

Store leather garments on strong wooden hangers to help the garments keep their shape.

Alteration & Repair. A regular tailor usually won't take leather alteration work. Ask your leather cleaner to recommend a tailor.

It is easier to take in leather than to let it out, because most manufacturers don't leave much of a seam allowance and, in any case, the old sewing needle marks would show.

Once leather has stretched, there is virtually nothing you can do to get it back to its original shape. Having a garment taken in is one option. But keep in mind that stretching changes the texture of leather, so the results may not be up to your expectations.

Whether a damaged garment can be repaired depends on the size of the rip. Small nicks can be glued. With an actual rip, however, the tailor must find leather that has a similar grain and color for a patch—which can be difficult.

Shoe care.

(See Page 125 for more tips.)

Advice from Mike Morelli, proprietor, Brooks Shoe Service, 55 East Washington Street, Suite 335, Chicago, IL, 60602, 312.372.2504; www.brooksshoeservice.com; call or e-mail for an estimate.

Weatherproofing. Weatherproof before polishing. Morelli recommends any of the silicone spray protectors (about $7) made for leather and suede, for your leather, suede and fabric shoes. Always check the product's label to make sure that it's safe for your type of shoe.

Before you treat any shoes, do a patch test in a hidden area.

If you get salt on your leather shoes, use a de-salter, which is available at shoe repair shops. Follow package directions.

If you don't have a de-salter, mix up a solution that is one part white vinegar and four parts water. Pour a small amount on a damp, clean cloth and wipe gently onto the shoes. If white salt stains are still visible, repeat the process. If the stains are still apparent after the second treatment, take the shoes to a professional.

If water has gotten inside your shoes, wipe them out and allow the shoes to dry completely. Never dry shoes on or near a heater. When shoes are two-thirds dry, put in shoe trees and let finish drying.

Water stains are tricky, and best professionally removed, but you can try what they use: Lincoln E-Z Cleaner (about $5), available at shoe repair shops. Follow package directions.

Making them last. Apply a thin rubber protective sole. According to Morelli, this can triple the life of your shoes. At Brooks, this service costs $23.50 and up for ladies and $25.50 and up for men's shoes.

Use shoe trees. Dasco shoe trees are one good brand. They makes trees for all shoe types, including sandals, slingbacks and boots.

CLEANING AND PROTECTION

Smooth leathers. To protect and polish smooth leathers, use Meltonian Boot and Shoe Cream Polish (about $3). Apply polish just often enough to keep the finish from looking worn or scuffed. Don't use too much polish—a dab will do it—and buff well.

In general, for soft, supple leathers, use a cream. For hard, stiff leathers that have a lot of body, use a wax polish such as Kiwi Shoe Polish (about $3), which offers good protection against water.

If you can't find polish in the color you need, use Meltonian's neutral. It's the cream polish without any color stain.

Most dirt and some spots can be removed with a slightly damp cloth. If that doesn't work, then try dabbing spots with just a little spot remover—such as AFTA or Kiwi's spot remover—on a clean white cloth.

Suede. Suede must be "dry" cleaned by brushing—not scrubbing—with a fine, flexible-bristle suede brush. (Morelli recommends Dasco, about $5.) Use after every third wearing, or whenever needed, to remove dust, dirt and scuff marks. Then spray lightly (three or four seconds) with shoe protector.

If you get moisture on your shoes, blot dry with a clean cloth.

For stains, use a suede eraser or suede stone, which looks like an art-gum eraser (about $4), available at shoe repair shops.

Next, try Lincoln E-Z Cleaner (see "Smooth leathers," at left) or use a touch of spot remover or take your shoes to a professional.

After its first professional cleaning, suede looks fine; after that, however, suede will begin to fade with every cleaning.

If your suede shoes get very wet, take them to a professional.

Patent leather. To clean patent leather, spray with Windex, Pledge or white vinegar diluted with water, and wipe with a soft, clean cloth.

For spots, Morelli recommends using a small amount of spot remover such as AFTA or Kiwi on a clean white rag. Gently dab, and then use a clean, dry cloth to wipe dry.

Do not use Vaseline on your patent leathers. It won't clean or condition them; it will just make them sticky.

It's important to put shoe trees in your patent leather shoes so they don't wrinkle.

Fabric. For stains on fabric shoes, put a little spot remover such as AFTA on a clean, white cloth and blot. Then blot with a dry cloth. If that doesn't work, take the shoe to a professional as soon as you can.

Satin. You can't restore the finish to a textile. If your satin shoes are worn or stained, consider having them re-dyed a darker color to hide the damage.

According to Morelli, if you have good quality satin shoes, a professional should be able to get out grass stains and dirt.

If your satin shoes get wet, take them to a professional.

Beaded. Shoes with delicate beadwork need to be handled very carefully. Beading can be repaired, but try to save the original beads.

To clean, use the softest clean horsehair brush you can find.

Exotics. Polish exotics as you would smooth leather (see "Smooth leathers," at left), using Meltonian cream in neutral, or in a matching colored polish to remove scuff marks.

Like smooth leather, exotics are fairly stain-resistant. Remove salt stains with de-salting liquid, and spots with just enough spot remover to slightly dampen a cloth, as you would with smooth leather shoes (see left).

Bag care.

(See Page 129 for more tips.)

Advice from Chris Moore, manager, Artbag, 1130 Madison Avenue, New York, 10028; 212.744.2720; www.artbag.com; call, e-mail or simply send in your bag for a free estimate.

CLEANING AND PROTECTION

Leather. To clean a leather bag, use a leather cleaner and gently rub with a soft white cotton cloth or cheesecloth.

To protect and polish leather bags, use Meltonian Boot and Shoe Cream Polish (about $3), in neutral, unless you want a matching colored polish to cover scuff marks. (Wax polish is too heavy for handbags.) Be sparing with the polish and buff until your cloth comes away clean; you don't want the polish to rub off onto your clothing.

Suede. To prevent suede from looking dull, gently brush with a horsehair or nylon brush.

To remove dust trapped in the nap, carefully skim the bag with the most gentle attachment on your vacuum cleaner.

For stains, try a suede eraser or suede stone, which looks like an art-gum eraser (about $4), available at shoe repair shops.

If water or anything wet spills onto suede, it is difficult to remove. Take the bag to a handbag specialist as soon as possible.

Patent leather. To clean patent leather, spray Windex, Pledge or white vinegar diluted with water onto a clean cloth and wipe the bag, then wipe dry with a soft, clean cloth.

Fabric. It is best to take fabric bags to a professional, as cleaning at home may discolor them. If you have to clean stains or salt at home, patch-test a small spot by dampening. If the color stays and the fabric doesn't ripple, then you can spot-clean by blotting with a clean, damp cloth. Afterward, stuff the bag with tissue paper to help maintain its shape. Air-dry away from heat.

Canvas should be cleaned by brushing—without water.

Exotics. Polish with a neutral cream polish like Meltonian every three to four months or as needed. Patch-test before applying all over. Do not use wax polish; it's too heavy for a fine handbag.

Have your exotic-skin bag professionally cleaned once a year to maintain luster and increase longevity.

If your exotic leather starts to flake, take it to a professional. If the flaking on a reptile bag is the glaze coming off, the bag can be reglazed, starting at about $100. If, for example, alligator is dried and cracked, it can be underlined (the leather lining is replaced), starting at about $125. Brown dust coming from a reptile bag means that the leather underneath the skin is disintegrating; that, too, can be fixed, starting at about $125.

Beaded. Beaded bags are sewn onto a frame. If the frame bends, it can be straightened, which usually costs about $75. If the frame is broken, the repair is very expensive. To remove the bag from the frame, solder the frame together, replate it and reattach the bag costs about $450 and up at Artbag.

If beads fall off, keep them to take to a professional for re-beading.

Embellished bags should be hand-cleaned by a professional bag specialist, not by the dry cleaners.

Storage. Stuff bags with acid-free tissue paper (do not overstuff) and place inside a flannel bag or an old, clean pillowcase. Then store upright in a cool place.

Place chain straps inside a bag, so they do not mark the outside.

Leather or cloth straps should be wrapped around a bag.

Do not store patent leather in plastic, as it breaks down the tanning process; also, if your home is warm, the plastic will adhere to the leather.

Satin and suede bags should be wrapped in acid-free tissue and laid flat in a cardboard box.

If your bag is delicate, store it in a box when not in use.

Dry cleaning primer.

Information from Alan Spielvogel, director of technical services, Neighborhood Cleaners Association, 252 West 29th Street, New York, NY 10001; 212.967.3002.

The process. Dry cleaning isn't really dry. Soiled clothes are immersed in a large washing machine filled with a liquid chemical solvent that contains virtually no water. This solvent is best at removing oil-soluble stains like grease or olive oil. Small water-soluble stains are removed during the pre-treating and/or post-spotting stage of cleaning. (Larger water-soluble stains may need to be removed during a process called wet cleaning, in which water and soap are used.) Once the garment is clean, it goes through a process called finishing, which reshapes it by machine pressing, hand-ironing or steaming.

STAINS

Stains can be removed with varying degrees of difficulty—depending on what caused them, how long they've been able to set and what types of fibers are involved. When they set a price or give an estimate, some cleaners factor in the extra time it takes to remove stains or treat clothing. For the best possible outcome, take stained clothing to your dry cleaners as soon as you can.

Oil-based. Stains made by oils, grease and lipstick do not wash out with soap. In fact, oil-based stains are often "set" by soap and water. If you get an oily substance on a garment, take it to a dry cleaner immediately.

Water-based. These include stains from drinks and perspiration. Blot dry and take to a cleaner within 24 hours.

Combination. These need to be treated first as an oily stain then as a water stain.

FABRICS

Generally, wool and cotton are fairly hardy. The following fabrics, however, are fragile. Always read the care instructions on your labels. Avoid applying perfume directly onto your clothing, because most perfumes contain alcohol and can destroy the fabric. The same is true of hair spray.

Silk. Silk is the most difficult fabric for cleaners to deal with. Interestingly, its weakness is caused by the gums and resins used to give it sheen.

Silk also has poor dye retention, so it discolors very easily.

Perspiration is the biggest problem for silk, because the amino acids and chlorine salts in perspiration cause the fabric to rot over time. Therefore, it is important to get silk cleaned after almost every wearing.

Spandex. All spandex eventually loses its elasticity; however, it usually lasts longer if you dryclean or hand-wash instead of putting it through a washer and dryer.

Spandex can break down or snap through wear or mechanical action during washing and cleaning. How much breakdown depends on the strength of the spandex fiber and the fiber with which it was blended. (If spandex is blended with strong fibers like cotton or wool, you'll see less stretching.)

Perspiration can discolor spandex or make it deteriorate more quickly—so you should wash or dryclean after every wearing.

Knits. Go by the care tag. Often, sweaters should only be washed by hand. Too much mechanical action or heat can damage a delicate knit. While there is less mechanical action involved in dry cleaning than in machine washing, dry cleaning may still be too harsh.

Embellished garments. There are dry cleaners that specialize in cleaning delicate garments. You should look for one before cleaning a specialty item.

Unusual garments should be tested before dry cleaning. After testing, a dry cleaner will put the garment in a net bag and use a very gentle cycle with little mechanical action.

If a garment has glued-on jeweled embellishment, the jewels should be taken off, because the dry cleaning process will dissolve the glue.

Some garments just can't be cleaned. Wedding gowns often can't be serviced.

PROBLEMS

Shine. Clothing develops shine due to abrasion, usually in areas where there is lots of wear (elbows, seat-of-the-pants). Unfortunately, this can't be avoided—especially in fabrics that are prone to abrasion, such as velour and gabardine.

Odors. If your clothes come back smelling like body odor or chemicals, change cleaners. Yours probably does not change their solvent often enough.

Ruined or lost clothing. Keep your receipts. If it's the dry cleaners' fault, they should reimburse you for the garment—but problems can occur because of a misprint on the care label. In that case, the manufacturer should reimburse you.

The amount of reimbursement is usually less than the cost of the garment itself, since the cleaner or manufacturer will take depreciation into account.

Cost. A woman's shirt often costs more to dryclean than a man's does, because women's garments are harder to press. The pressing machine can accommodate only basic business dress shirts. If a woman's shirt is cut like a man's, the price should be the same. However, if her shirt has darts, appliqués or ruffles, the price goes up, because additional labor is required to hand-iron the piece. This also applies to childrens' shirts or men's tuxedo or Hawaiian shirts (i.e., fuller shirts).

APPENDIX 4

Clothing storage.

Everyday storage. After wearing, air out clothes for an hour or overnight before putting them in a closet.

Cedar hangers, which are thick and absorb moisture, are the best choice for hanging your clothes. Wire hangers are the worst. If you must use wire hangers, use them only for hanging lightweight shirts or blouses without shoulder pads.

For blouses with shoulder pads, dresses and lightweight jackets, use wide plastic or padded hangers.

Tailored pieces—like suit jackets, winter coats and heavier pieces—need padded or wood hangers.

It is best to hang slacks and skirts from the waist by clips.

If you fold pants over a hanger, be sure to readjust them every once in while, as they collect dust and fade at the point of folding.

Knits should be folded, not hung, in order to avoid stretching.

Seasonal storage. Clothing that you put into short-term storage needs to be protected from insects, humidity, heat, fading, odors, and pollution. You need to find a dark, dry, well-ventilated area in your home that remains at a fairly constant temperature.

Clean everything before you put it in storage. Insects are attracted to dirt and odors. Also, invisible spills can oxidize into permanent stains.

Store clothes on sturdy, wide hangers or folded with tissue paper. Do not wrap in plastic, as it traps moisture. Instead, cover everything in canvas bags, which are available at home stores.

Cedar chests and closets are optimal for storage. If you don't have either, add cedar chips to your storage bags. (When cedar loses its fragrance, it's no longer effective. Buy new chips, and sand cedar closets or chest walls to expose fresh wood.) Mothballs do their job well, but produce an odor that is hard to remove from clothing.

If you can't store at home, consider using your dry cleaners for storing woolens and coats and a specialty facility for storing items such as furs, antique clothing and highly embellished pieces.